# ESSENTIAL
# Charles Rennie Mackintosh

# ESSENTIAL

# Charles Rennie Mackintosh

Fanny Blake

This is a Parragon Book
First published in 2001

Parragon
Queen Street House
4 Queen Street
Bath BA1 1HE, UK

ISBN: 0-75255-351-8

A copy of the CIP data for this book is available from the
British Library upon request.

The right of Fanny Blake to be identified as the author
of this work has been asserted in accordance with
Section 77 of the Copyright, Designs and Patents Act
of 1988.

Editorial, design and layout by Essential Books,
7 Stucley Place, London NW1 8NS

Picture research: Image Select International

Printed and bound in China

# CONTENTS

# INTRODUCTION

Charles Rennie Mackintosh has become an international phenomenon in recent years, one of Glasgow's greatest exports. It is ironic, then, that during his lifetime he received scant recognition at home, finding greater popularity for his designs in Europe than in his own country. His reputation was founded not on his architectural designs alone but also on his interiors, which demonstrated his ability to integrate furniture with its setting. To him, his role as an architect encompassed fine art and craft as well, the relationship between the three being inextricable. Mackintosh's range of achievement was superb. He worked in public, commercial and domestic environments, and designed well over four hundred pieces of furniture. He produced Symbolist paintings, detailed botanical sketches and landscapes. Yet most of his major work was completed in just over a decade, between 1896 and 1909.

Mackintosh was one of eleven children born to William McIntosh, a clerk in the police force, and Margaret Rennie McIntosh. His father was an upright member of the community with a passion for gardening. This he encouraged in his son, with the result that Mackintosh sketched flowers throughout his life.

When he was sixteen Mackintosh became a pupil with an architect, John Hutchison, who ran a small practice in the centre of Glasgow. At this time the city was booming, not only industrially but also in the world of the arts. A group of local artists known as the Glasgow Boys were being noticed at home and abroad. Links with the Pre-Raphaelites, an awareness of the British Arts and Crafts movement, a fashion for Japanese art, and knowledge of work by artists both in Britain and on the Continent meant change was in the air. As in so many cities, the favoured architectural style in the first half of the nineteenth century had been Neoclassical. By the 1850s that was changing in most places, but not in Glasgow. Thanks largely to the work of architect Alexander Thomson, many Glaswegian buildings were still being constructed in the Greek

Revival style and it was not until his death in 1875 that things really began to change, with other influences finding their way in.

In 1883, like so many keen young architects of the time, Mackintosh had begun to attend classes at the Glasgow School of Art. In 1885 an Englishman, Francis Newbery, was appointed its director. Acutely aware of current trends in the arts, he was determined to make the school a success by moving away from its political origins and recognizing and fostering individual talent. He supported Mackintosh's career from these early days, becoming a lifelong friend and support.

Mackintosh joined Honeyman and Keppie as an assistant architect in 1889. He worked principally with the young Keppie, a man who had recently been brought in to breathe new life into the partnership. In 1891 Mackintosh delivered a lecture to the Glasgow Architectural Association entitled 'Scottish Baronial Architecture' in which he made a forceful case for using a vernacular style but adapting it to modern needs. Later that year, having won the prestigious Alexander Thomson Travelling Scholarship in 1890 for his design for a public hall, he went to Italy. He had never been out of the country before and used the scholarship money to travel from city to city, sketching and painting the buildings that impressed him. The experience didn't apparently influence his own work but it must have considerably enhanced his status in local architectural circles when he returned home.

In the early days Keppie used his assistant on a range of projects, including the refurbishment of the interiors of Craigie Hall and the Glasgow Art Club, where Mackintosh's hand can be seen distinctly in the detail of the wooden carvings. It was around this time that his interests broadened into the worlds of fine and decorative arts. He had a close relationship with Jessie Keppie, John's sister, and she probably introduced both him and fellow draughtsman Herbert McNair to a group of women art students who called themselves the Immortals. Among them were Frances and Margaret Macdonald, with whom the young men began to work closely, developing a symbolic vocabulary so obscure that it has now become impossible to interpret accurately. They became known as the Four, developing a distinctive style of painting which was showcased in the Immortals' publication, *The Magazine*. Their work frequently featured long-haired, etiolated women whose weird, ghoul-like presence earned the small group the nickname 'the Spook School'.

In 1895 Mackintosh designed the Martyrs' Public School and also produced his Symbolist watercolours *The Tree of Influence – The Tree of Importance – The Sun of Cowardice* and *The Tree of Personal Effort – The Sun of Indifference*. Soon after, he turned his hand to a new area, poster art, both as a member of the Four and on his own, producing huge arresting posters that were designed to shock – and shock they did. By this time Mackintosh considered himself very much an artist–architect, as his photographic portrait taken in 1893 shows.

Mackintosh's architectural work had continued to develop. In 1893 he was heavily involved with the additions to the Glasgow Herald Building, which clearly carries his signature in the tower and the arrangement of windows on the Mitchell Street façade. The following years saw him working on Queen Margaret's Medical College and the Martyrs' Public School. Then, in 1896, Honeyman and Keppie were invited to compete for the design of a new Glasgow School of Art on a tricky sloping site in Renfield Street. While working on this, Mackintosh exhibited with the Macdonald sisters at the Arts and Crafts Exhibition in London. Their watercolours, furniture and metalwork met with a mixed reception, ranging from approval through indifference to outright scorn. They were never invited to exhibit as a foursome in England again. This was also the year that Mackintosh was invited to join a young interior designer, George Walton, and come up with stencilled murals for Miss Cranston's Buchanan Street Tea Rooms. This marked the beginning of a long and fruitful relationship, with Mackintosh creating a series of spectacular interiors for Miss Cranston's growing number of establishments.

Early the following year, his designs for Queen's Cross Church were approved. Then it was announced that Honeyman and Keppie had won the commission for the Glasgow School of Art. Though the job was run by Keppie, there is no doubt that the design was Mackintosh's and it was to prove his masterwork. The first phase of building continued from 1896 to 1899. During this period, he also refurbished the interiors for Miss Cranston's Argyle Street Tea Rooms, with George Walton responsible for the wall decoration. Of all the furniture Mackintosh had designed to date, the high-backed chair for these tea rooms must be the most remarkable.

When Herbert McNair was appointed Instructor of Decorative Design at Liverpool University in 1898, the collaborative days of the Four were numbered. McNair married Frances Macdonald and they went to live in Merseyside. In 1900 Mackintosh married Margaret. From then on she created little work on her own but collaborated extensively with her husband, so much so that it is impossible to know exactly how much of his designs should be credited to her. This was the time when Mackintosh's work was at its peak. The first phase of the Glasgow School of Art had been completed, he had designed the Queen's Cross Church, which was built by 1899, and was heavily involved with the design of the new Daily Record Building, remarkable for its white-glazed brick exterior.

That year he received his first commission to design a detached family home for William Davidson, a local businessman. This, together with the Hill House for William Blackie (1902–4), at last gave him the opportunity to put his design theories into practice, creating bold new buildings with their roots in Scottish traditional architecture. As importantly, he and Margaret moved into a flat in Mains Street which they had thoroughly renovated. It is one of their most important interiors. In 1898 Mackintosh had designed his first white bedroom at Westdel for Robert Maclehose, but at last he and Margaret were unrestrained by any client's demands. They were free to create their white rooms exactly as they dreamed them – stark, spacious, light, and in complete contrast to most interiors of the time. Meanwhile, Miss Cranston had purchased several buildings in Ingram Street. George Walton had by now moved away from Glasgow, so Mackintosh had the whole commission for these interiors to himself. He based his designs on what he and Margaret had done at Mains Street, and transferred them successfully from a domestic to a commercial setting.

In November, the Four were invited to take part in the Vienna Secession Exhibition. The Mackintoshes designed a white room, similar to their Mains Street flat and including some of the same furniture designs. For Mackintosh, the trip was thrilling. Not only did it take his work to a new and enthusiastic audience but it also put him in touch with Europe's avant-garde design movement, an influence seen in his later work. While there, they may have heard of the competition to design a notional country retreat for an art lover. Mackintosh entered a scheme, and although he was disqualified for failing to submit the correct number of interior perspectives, he did receive a prize and his drawings were published. Although the house was never built in his lifetime, it has now been realised in Bellahouston Park, outside Glasgow. Mackintosh's conception of a magnificent music room within the house may have led Fritz Wärndorfer, patron of the Viennese Secession, to commission his own music room from him. Then, in 1902, the Mackintoshes created the exquisite Rose Boudoir for the Turin International Exhibition, which led to invitations to exhibit in Dresden, Moscow and Berlin.

This decade was Mackintosh's most successful and productive. He was designing the Hill House, his finest domestic commission, and also his most elaborate tea room yet, the Willow Tea Rooms in Sauchiehall Street. In 1903 he was asked to design a new board school in Scotland Street. Despite being constrained by a tight budget, he came up with a wonderfully innovative scheme incorporating two glass towers. The same year he completed the interiors for the Hill House, including its unique furnishings, and Miss Cranston asked him to refurbish her home, Hous'hill. Then in 1905 he started work on a house for F. J. Shand at Auchinibert in Stirlingshire; the house was completed in 1908.

In 1906, the Mackintoshes bought their own house in Glasgow's West End. They used much of their old furniture and an interior design similar to that in their Mains Street flat. The house has been reconstructed by the Hunterian Art Gallery and today provides a strong sense of what their domestic life must have been like. In 1907 the board of governors of the Glasgow School of Art decided to fund the completion of the original design. Mackintosh reworked his plans for the west wing, producing his undoubted architectural masterpiece.

Mackintosh was now at the peak of his career, but curiously, apart from a few tea rooms commissioned by Miss Cranston, he completed little other architectural work. A difficult and demanding man professionally, he had become consumed by depression and drink. Eventually, in 1913, he resigned from Honeyman and Keppie for reasons that are unclear. He attempted to set up on his own but failed to get any work.

The following year, he and Margaret travelled to Walberswick in Suffolk, where Francis Newbery had a holiday home. They rented the house next door, planning to stay until Mackintosh was fully rested. However, the First World War broke out three weeks after their arrival and they decided to stay on. Mackintosh began to recuperate and completed a number of exquisite botanical watercolours which were destined for publication in Germany. The book never materialised, but over forty of the paintings survive.

The Mackintoshes' stay in Walberswick was cut short when Mackintosh was accused of being a German spy and ordered to leave the area. Both he and Margaret were distraught at the turn of events and Mackintosh travelled to London to clear his name. When Margaret joined him, they settled in a small flat in Glebe Place, Chelsea, each with their own studio nearby. Architectural work was thin on the ground but in 1914, soon after moving into Glebe Place, Mackinstosh was tracked down by W. J. Bassett-Lowke, who had heard of his reputation from a friend in Cornwall. Bassett-Lowke was moving into a terraced house at 78 Derngate, Northampton, and asked Mackintosh to enlarge the interior space and create a bathroom. Mackintosh responded with one of the most startling design schemes of his career. Bright and colourful, relying on geometric patterns, it seems to owe its inspiration to the work of the Vienna Secession.

At this time, the Mackintoshes supplemented their meagre income by textile design. Their work was much influenced by avant-garde movements in the arts and their principal customers were the large firms of William Foxton's and Sefton's.

In 1916 Mackintosh completed his final designs for Miss Cranston, who wanted a basement addition to her Willow Tea Rooms. Patriotically named the Dug Out, it followed the same formula as 78 Derngate with its rich geometric pattern against black walls and ceiling. This was his last significant work. Between 1917 and 1920 he had some minor commissions from Bassett-Lowke and in 1920 he designed studio houses for the painters Harold Squire and Arthur Cadogan Blunt and studios for the sculptor Francis Derwent Wood. All these were to be in Glebe Place, but only the one for Harold Squire was realised. Later in the year he designed a block of studios and studio flats in Cheyne Walk for the Arts League of Service, together with a theatre that the dancer Margaret Morris proposed for the same area. Neither of these projects was built, however. It was a sad time for Mackintosh. Buoyed up by the prospect of designing five new buildings, he must have felt extremely let down to see only one heavily modified version completed. The drawings and sketches of the others that survive show his enduring fascination with the square and the influence of Vienna.

In 1923 the Mackintoshes left for a holiday in France. They were to remain there for four years, travelling round the Pyrenees, staying in cheap hotels and enjoying the simple life. During this time Mackintosh produced a series of watercolours very different from anything he had attempted before. Preoccupied by the landscape, Mackintosh enjoyed dramatic perspectives of rocks, villages and hillsides. These paintings are static, unpeopled and frequently reduce the elements of landscape to abstraction.

In 1927 Margaret was forced to return to London for medical reasons. Mackintosh's letters show him relaxed, not drinking and struggling to establish a painting style for himself. They also complain of a sore tongue, which was diagnosed in London the following year as cancer. The Mackintoshes stayed in London for treatment, but this was unsuccessful and Mackintosh was eventually admitted to a nursing home, where he died in 1928. After his death Margaret continued to travel, staying in a succession of small hotels in England and France. Eventually, in 1933, she returned to Chelsea, where she died.

After her death, the Mackintoshes' remaining possessions were valued at just under £90. In the last few years, though, a single high-backed chair has fetched over £300,000 at auction. Mackintosh's work is now recognised as being expressive of its time. It both reflected what had gone before and anticipated designs that were to become fashionable years later. He has now achieved the recognition in his city that he lacked during his life. On visiting Glasgow, it is impossible not to be aware of his existence. Near the Glasgow School of Art , the Willow Tea Rooms have been restored and still contain many original features. The Queen's Cross Church is home to the Charles Rennie Mackintosh Society, while the Glasgow Herald Building has become the Lighthouse, a centre for architecture and design. The Mackintoshes' house at 78 Southpark Avenue has been meticulously reconstructed in the Hunterian Art Gallery, while the Hill House at Helensburgh belongs to the National Trust for Scotland. Work still goes on in Mackintosh's name. The House for an Art Lover has been built in Bellahouston Park, almost a century after its conception, and plans are afoot to reconstruct the Ingram Street Tea Rooms some thirty years after they were dismantled. Whether his claim to be Scotland's greatest architect will be sustained cannot be known, but his name will never be forgotten.

# CHARLES RENNIE MACKINTOSH *1868–1928*

## PORTRAIT

*Courtesy of T. & R. Annan & Sons*

IN 1893, when this photograph was taken, Mackintosh's life was changing. The son of a police clerk, he was now an architect with the Glasgow firm of Honeyman and Keppie. This was the year in which he had his first large commission, the design of new warehousing for the prestigious local newspaper the *Glasgow Herald*. He also designed his first suite of furniture as a wedding present for his friend David Gauld. In the evenings he also found time to attend classes at the Glasgow School of Art, since he was already convinced that the worlds of art, architecture and craft were interlinked and inseparable.

Mackintosh was at this time engaged to Jessie Keppie, whose brother John was a partner at his firm. Jessie attended the School of Art during the day and was probably the one who introduced Mackintosh and his friend Herbert McNair to the Immortals, a group of young women art students. Among these students were Margaret and Frances Macdonald, two sisters who were to have a profound influence on Mackintosh's and McNair's lives and careers. In this photograph, Mackintosh deliberately presents himself not as a professional working architect but as an artist, the loose cravat, the self-conscious kiss curl on his forehead and the wistful gaze all consciously announcing his new identity.

## MARGARET MACDONALD *1863–1933*

### PORTRAIT

*Courtesy of the Hunterian Art Gallery, University of Glasgow*

MARGARET Macdonald was born in Newcastle under Lyme. She met Charles Rennie Mackintosh in 1893 at the Glasgow School of Art, where she and her sister, Frances, were part of the group known as the Immortals. In 1895 the two sisters opened a studio in Hope Street, near the studio of Herbert McNair, a friend of Mackintosh. In the previous year the Four, as they became known, had exhibited at the Institute of Fine Art, where their strange, dreamy designs attracted considerable attention. Their distinctive style took its inspiration from the work of, among others, Aubrey Beardsley, Jan Toorop and the Pre-Raphaelites, and they evolved a complex symbolic vocabulary entirely of their own.

A talented artist in her own right, Margaret had great influence on Mackintosh's development and after their marriage in 1900 much of their work was inextricably linked. Exactly how closely she collaborated with Mackintosh on his interiors is unclear, but he frequently added her initials to his when he signed his drawings. Particularly notable are the decorative gesso panels she designed for the Willow Tea Rooms (1904) and the Wärndorfer Music Salon in Vienna and the embroidered panels that feature in some of his other interiors.

His devoted companion and muse throughout their lives together, Margaret survived Mackintosh by five years.

# CRAIGIE HALL,
## BELLAHOUSTON PARK, GLASGOW *1892–3*

### DETAIL OF WOOD CARVING ON BENCH END

*Courtesy of Eric Thorburn*

MACKINTOSH joined the Glasgow firm of Honeyman and Keppie in 1889 as an assistant architect. Already recognised as being a talented designer, his hand can be seen clearly in some of the firm's commissions in his early years there, even though his name did not appear on them at this stage.

Honeyman had established his architectural practice some years earlier and, wanting to inject new blood into the firm, had appointed the young John Keppie as his partner in the 1888. Keppie was only seven years older than Mackintosh and, to begin with, Mackintosh worked closely with him. Keppie often took charge of their joint projects but seems to have left much − if not all − of the detail to the younger man.

In 1872, John Honeyman had designed Craigie Hall for Thomas Mason, a successful local builder. Now, 20 years later, John Keppie was entrusted with carrying out a series of alterations to the entrance and the library at Craigie Hall. The detailed carving on this bench end clearly shows Mackintosh's work in the face of a long-haired, dreamy woman, as it merges with and is surrounded by natural forms of foliage and flowers which lend a fluidity to the design in the unmistakable 'Spook School' style. There is no evidence of Keppie being a student of this style, thus it is clearly Mackintosh's work. He manages to complement, rather than clash with, the detailing on the mirrors that are positioned above the bench, while making a strong, modern statement in style.

# GLASGOW HERALD BUILDING, MITCHELL STREET, GLASGOW *1893*

## FAÇADE

*Courtesy of Eric Thorburn*

IN 1893 Honeyman and Keppie were asked to build a new warehouse at the back of the *Glasgow Herald*'s existing building on a corner site in Mitchell Street. Mackintosh was only an assistant in the firm, but his designs were used. What is particularly striking about this façade is the balance of tension he achieves between the horizontal and the vertical. The windows are treated in horizontal bands which, on the ground, first, second and third floors, run around the building uninterrupted, only changing as the upward thrust of the tower takes over.

The warehouse building is typically Scottish baronial in appearance but for the games Mackintosh played with the windows. Internally, the first, second and third floors were identically laid out, but Mackintosh gave them each different windows, though always setting back the small timber-framed sashes to show the thickness of the walls. The square-paned glazing is constant, but the shapes of the windows tell a different story. The first two floors are given greater importance than those above. He played with the window shapes in the central staircase bay, each one different in size and surround: a negative architrave, different sills, a triangular pediment that is repeated in the gable ends, a curved pediment anticipating those above. The cornice suggests the roof will be immediately above, but instead two more floors rise up before the roof is reached with its gables at either end. Mackintosh took the elements of classical architecture but treated them in an unorthodox way, showing his affiliation to the new Free Style then coming to the fore. Today the building is no longer used by the *Glasgow Herald*, but it was instead reopened in 1999 as the Lighthouse, a centre devoted to architecture and design.

## GLASGOW HERALD BUILDING *1893*

# TOWER

*Courtesy of Eric Thorburn*

AMONG their other requirements, the owners specified a water tower as a precaution against fire, and it is unquestionably Mackintosh's signature on this grandiose structure that dominates the street.

The tower rises over 150 feet to hide the 8,000-gallon water tank within it. Its design is possibly based on the architecture which Mackintosh sketched on his Italian trip, for features such as the pilasters on the corners resemble those on the clock tower in Siena. However, the elaborate detailing also recalls the Scottish baronial style which is frequently reflected in Mackintosh's work and evidence of his desire to retain elements of tradition in what was a basically modern style.

The windows change in style as the tower rises to its upper limits. On the first four floors, they continue around, identical in appearance to those on the Mitchell Street façade. As the contrast and tension develop between the upward thrust of the tower and the horizontal movement of the main body of the building, the positioning of the windows becomes asymmetrical. At a higher stage still, the corners of the windowless level are ornamented with curious tongue-like shapes before the tower rises another two storeys to be crowned with an ogee roof, similar to the ones Mackintosh would later use for the Martyrs' Public School and in his design for Queen Margaret's Medical College.

# MARTYRS' PUBLIC SCHOOL, 11 PARSON STREET, GLASGOW 1895–7

## PERSPECTIVE DRAWING

*Courtesy of the Hunterian Art Gallery,
University of Glasgow*

CHANGES in the laws affecting education meant there was a great call at the end of the nineteenth century for architects to design new schools. The Martyrs' Public School was the first of two such commissions for Mackintosh. The school board wanted a school for a thousand students built along traditional lines, with segregated entrances and stairs at the east and west, a central hall, and three floors of standard classrooms. No doubt because of the tight budget, the building is largely unremarkable but for the three large staircase windows with the arch and corbelled sills giving relief to an otherwise severe façade. However, Mackintosh's signature appears in other subtle ways. The architrave on the doors anticipates his design for the Glasgow School of Art, while inside details of metalwork and tiling foreshadow later designs. The roof trusses over the stairs look as if they are influenced by Japanese building design, the uprights appearing to be held by two horizontal beams. It is known that Mackintosh read Edward S. Morse's *Japanese Homes and Their Surroundings* (1886). In fact, the beam ends turn out to be nothing more than small carved pieces of wood tacked on to an upright. Mackintosh's enthusiasm was for the finished appearance, not the exact replication of their structure. The same influence is apparent in the timber eaves that jut out over the stairwell windows. The stern institutional appearance of the building is relieved by his use of the white octagonal ogee roofs, which disguise the ventilation outlets but also underline the fact that the apparently separate sections of the building all belong to the same institution.

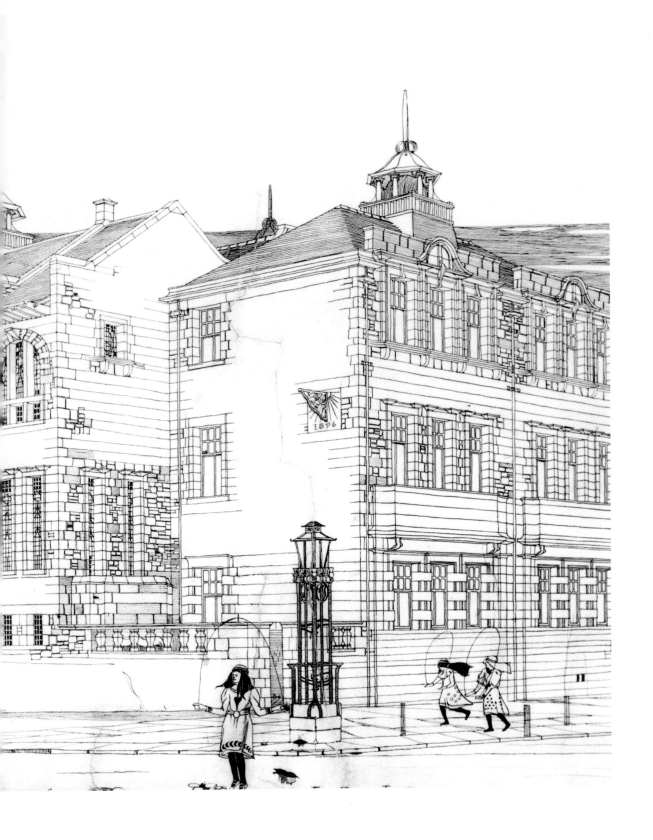

# MISS CATHERINE CRANSTON *(1849–1934)*

## PORTRAIT

*Courtesy of T. & R. Annan & Sons*

GLASGOW was a thriving commercial centre in the second half of the nineteenth century. The temperance movement was powerful in a city renowned for its fondness for a wee dram. Its catering was as celebrated, with baking and lunch rooms known far beyond the confines of the city. The advent of the tea room was a blessing for those who wanted light refreshment without the temptation of strong drink, and by 1897, Glasgow had been dubbed 'a veritable Tokyo of tea rooms'.

Stuart Cranston had a chain of six tea rooms and many other independents had sprung up, mainly run by women. Cranston's main competitor was none other than his own sister, Catherine. A small, determined woman who insisted on wearing Victorian costume that was at least thirty years out of date, she provided formidable competition. She opened her first tea room at 114 Argyle Street in 1878, followed by another in Ingram Street in 1886. The important thing about the tea rooms was that they were decorated in a domestic way to make people feel comfortable, even though Catherine favoured the latest fashions in the decorative arts. A perfectionist, she insisted on every detail conforming exactly to her overall plan. When she decided to redecorate her Argyle Street Tea Rooms in 1888, she employed a young designer, George Walton. He was involved in her next scheme in Buchanan Street when Mackintosh was asked to come up with the stencilled murals.

This was to be the beginning of a long and fruitful relationship with Miss Cranston. Mackintosh designed all her tea rooms from then on and was even trusted with the refurbishment of her home, Hous'hill.

## MISS CRANSTON'S
## BUCHANAN STREET TEA ROOMS *1896*

## STENCILLED MURAL DECORATION
## FOR THE LUNCH GALLERY

*Courtesy of the Hunterian Art Gallery,*
*University of Glasgow*

A phenomenon peculiar to Glasgow, tea rooms sprang up during the 1880s and 1890s. Principally responsible was the redoubtable Miss Cranston, who pioneered the fashion, providing sanctuary for God-fearing folk away from the mean streets of Glasgow. By 1895 she already had two successful tea rooms in Argyle Street and Ingram Street; it was time to build a new one in Buchanan Street, Glasgow's fashionable shopping street. She was only too aware of the attraction of good interior design and put a young Glaswegian designer, George Walton, in charge. It is not known whether she or he invited Mackintosh to provide mural decorations on three floors for the lunch room, the lunch gallery and the smoking gallery above.

In any event, it was here that he was able to demonstrate publicly his belief in the interior as a work of art. In the lunch gallery he designed a stencilled mural which was composed of tall women in the 'Spook School' style apparently entwined in rose bushes and turned towards a curious tree-like form which, it has been suggested, has sexual connotations. Resembling much of the figurative work of the Four, the private symbolism of these images remains unknown but there is no doubt that they caused considerable controversy.

## MISS CRANSTON'S BUCHANAN STREET TEA ROOMS *1897–8*

# PEACOCK STUDY

*Courtesy of the Hunterian Art Gallery, University of Glasgow*

MACKINTOSH'S designs for the Buchanan Street Tea Rooms in Glasgow were highly individualistic and presented Miss Cranston's staid Glaswegian customers with what must have been, to some of them at least, a startling glimpse of what was new in the world of decorative art. Startled as they may have been, however, it is highly unlikely that these members of the public would have understood the work they saw there on any other than the most superficial level. They may have enjoyed their surroundings, but the private symbolism contained in the tea rooms was really known only to the Four.

From the lower gallery of the tea rooms, it was possible to see all three floors, so Mackintosh unified his scheme by using green at the bottom, a greyish-greenish yellow in the middle and blue at the top, apparently in order to represent the move from earth to heaven. Above the lunch gallery, he decorated the smoking room with a mural of clouds. In the luncheon room below, he used an elegant design of green and black peacocks standing between stylised trees.

This was Mackintosh's first opportunity to design mural decoration on such a huge scale. What he achieved on this site was unlike anything that had been seen in a tea room before, giving the Buchanan Street premises a notoriety and particular cachet all of their own.

# GLASGOW SCHOOL OF ART, 167 RENFREW STREET, GLASGOW *1896–9, 1907–9*

## NORTH FAÇADE 1896–9

*Courtesy of Mark Fiennes/Arcaid*

IN 1885 the governors of the Glasgow School of Art appointed Francis Newbery as its new director. He was ambitious for the school and its pupils and proved a lifelong supporter of Mackintosh's work. The school occupied cramped premises in Sauchiehall Street, but in 1895 a plot was acquired in Renfrew Street and various firms of architects were invited to compete for the job of designing a new school. Newbery and his governors provided an explicit brief, detailing the size of the studios, their need for northern light and the specifics of the windows. There were to be wide corridors with plenty of wall space for exhibiting work, electric light, good ventilation and perhaps a museum for displaying sculptures. To avoid any criticism of extravagance, they also insisted on a tight budget. Honeyman and Keppie won the competition. Although it is accepted that Mackintosh drew up the scheme, Keppie's name was attached to the job. The north façade exactly reflects the internal plan of the building, resulting in a masterpiece of balanced asymmetry. The entrance is at the centre of the building, though to one side of the central section, which houses the administrative offices. The janitor's office occupies the ground floor of the oriel bay, which is reminiscent of houses sketched by Mackintosh in Lyme Regis. Above the door, the director's office has an impressive balcony which links it with the bay beside it and the grand pediment above. Slightly incongruously, to one side and over the janitor's office, is the director's lavatory. The floor above is taken up with the director's studio. To each side of this section stretch the studios, divided internally by movable screens. The austerity of the window design, no architrave and the most simple of lintels and reveals, contrasts with the complex asymmetry of the whole façade. On the east side are three windows, each five panes wide. To the west are four windows, two of them five panes wide and two of them only four. The overhanging roof hides the view of the upper studios from the street.

## GLASGOW SCHOOL OF ART *1896–9*

# DETAIL OF WINDOW BRACKETS

*Courtesy of the Glasgow Picture Library*

THE face of the north side of the Glasgow School of Art building is somewhat stern and utilitarian. This harshness is relieved, however, by Mackintosh's highly imaginative use of wrought ironwork. The huge studio windows are braced by decorative metal brackets, which were designed with the additional and practical purpose of supporting window-cleaners' planks.

The head of each of these decorative brackets is an intricate whorl of metal, the form of which subtly changes from window to window. On the east side of the building, moving outwards from the centre window, the three sets of brackets represent the growth of a seed: the first set contains a stamen-like shape, the second a tiny seed and the third a plump, mature seed. And on the west side of the building, the heads of the brackets represent flowers similar in form to the stylised roses that appear so frequently elsewhere in Mackintosh's work.

Mackintosh's use of organic forms to signify the notion of growth is entirely appropriate here, within the context of an educational institution. The brackets also add another visual dimension to the building as they appear reflected in the windows or cast their shadows dramatically across the stonework, their curves softening the otherwise severe lines of the façade.

GLASGOW SCHOOL OF ART *1896–9*

# MAIN ENTRANCE:
## NORTH FAÇADE

*Courtesy of Mark Fiennes/Arcaid*

THE main entrance to the Glasgow School of Art is positioned exactly at the midpoint of the north façade. Placed at the dead centre of the entrance is a wooden post with a wide head that touches the lintel. Originally the doors stood at the back of the porch, leaving the post standing alone like a boundary marker or possibly a symbolic tree of knowledge – the latter particularly suitable at the entrance to a place of learning.

The entrance itself is framed by a curved architrave. The mouldings around it culminate in the stone relief above the door, where two female figures, the guardians of the building, sit on either side of a stylised tree. The forms of these figures are so intricately related to the building that it is hard to say where the moulding stops and the architecture begins.

The design of these female figures is clearly linked to the work of the Four. Together the Four had developed and evolved a style of figurative and symbolic representation which held meanings unknown to anyone outside their own enlightened circle. Mackintosh was a firm believer in the inextricable unity of art, architecture, craft and nature and he modelled the initial maquette for this stone carving himself.

## GLASGOW SCHOOL OF ART *1896–9*

# DETAIL OF RAILINGS OUTSIDE NORTH FAÇADE

*Courtesy of David Churchill/Arcaid*

FURTHER striking use of wrought ironwork can be seen on the railings in front of the north side of the building. Unlike the façade itself, the arrangement of the wall and railings is quite symmetrical. However, the line of the railings is broken no fewer than eight times by groups of leafed stems pointing skywards.

From the midst of each group emerges a single stalk topped by a curious pierced metal disc. Each of these discs is different, once again adding to the sense of dislocation already established by the balanced asymmetry of the façade itself. There is no doubt that these symbols are based on Japanese *mon* or heraldic shields, which can be found documented in the Japanese section of the school's library. They seem to be stylised insect, plant or bird forms, but their exact meaning is not always clear.

This fascination of Mackintosh's with Japanese art and design emerges through much of his work, as does his symbolic use of natural forms. Japanese art was becoming fashionable at this time and prints were readily available throughout Britain; some can be seen against the walls in photographs of his flat in Mains Street.

Natural symbolism was a feature of Mackintosh's work that he had begun to develop with the Four and it subsequently reappeared frequently in both his interior and exterior designs. Much of it seemed almost eerie in execution and, viewed from the distance of time, quite idiosyncratic. One has to remember how modern it was considered at the time of Mackintosh's work.

## GLASGOW SCHOOL OF ART *1896–9*

# NORTH FACADE. FINIAL ABOVE DIRECTOR'S OFFICE

*Courtesy of Eric Thorburn / Glasgow Picture Library*

WHILE Mackintosh used wrought iron to splendid effect on the northern façade of the building, at the top of the tower containing the director's office and on the top of the east tower are two iron finials, symbolic representations of the city of Glasgow's coat of arms.

These finials are purely decorative flourishes and despite their appearance they do not have any functional use as weathervanes. The bird, the bell and the tree which feature in the finials all refer to various miracles performed by St Mungo (also known as St Kentigern), the patron saint of Glasgow. They also perfectly allow Mackintosh to indulge his interest in natural, spiritual and modern matters to great effect.

The tree depicted in Glasgow's coat of arms is a mature oak, but it started out as a branch of hazel. Legend says that St Mungo was in charge of a holy fire in St Serf's monastery when he fell asleep. Some boys who were envious of his favoured position with St Serf put out the fire, but St Mungo broke off frozen branches from a hazel tree nearby and, by dint of praying over them, caused them to burst into flames.

The bird represents a wild robin that was tamed by St Serf but then killed by St Mungo's jealous fellow students, intending that he should be blamed for the death. However, St Mungo is said to have taken the dead bird, prayed over it and miraculously restored it to life.

## GLASGOW SCHOOL OF ART *1896–9*

## EAST FAÇADE

*Courtesy of Eric Thorburn / Glasgow Picture Library*

A deliberately placed drainpipe neatly divides the east façade in half. To one side, the return wall of the north façade rises stark and monumental (the two lower windows are later additions). It was specified in the governors' brief that the studios should be lit only from the north, but even so another architect might have been tempted to relieve the void with some form of carving or decoration. On the other side, the wall is punctuated by symmetrically balanced windows, though typically of varying shapes and sizes. The janitor's accommodation (as was) is lit by the bottom two rows of windows. Above them is the staff-room window, whose pediment echoes the one over the director's office on the north side. Higher still, sharing a lintel, are the convex double windows to the boardroom. Beside them an oriel window lights the school wardrobe, which provides the base for the stair tower that juts upwards, a feature reminiscent of traditional Scottish baronial architecture. The upward sweep of the wall ends is complemented by the curved top of the low wall above, which is set back and was designed to have a relief of the city arms that never materialised. Few other modifications were made to Mackintosh's original design. Gable walls were levelled at the summit of the north side and a dovecote was transmuted into a birdhouse with a landing perch. At the base, the original drawing shows three trees which would have broken up the expanse of stone, but they were never planted.

## GLASGOW SCHOOL OF ART *1896–9*

# ENTRANCE HALL

*Courtesy of Mark Fiennes / Arcaid*

FOR Mackintosh, the entrance was a transitional area between the outside world and the interior of the building. His halls invite visitors in, his use of light drawing them towards the rooms or stairways beyond. In the Glasgow School of Art, the outside steps channel them through into a small vestibule by the janitor's office, then into the vaulted entrance hall. The hall is dark but the light streaming down the stairwell entices visitors further into the building. At the foot of the main staircase is the janitor's inquiry box, strategically placed at a point where he can see both the entrance and down the main corridor and, as importantly, be seen. However, it is the staircase itself that has generated most interest. Here Mackintosh plays with horizontal and vertical planes. The newel posts on either side of the inquiry box rise to the ceiling. At the back of the flight of stairs, two newel posts reach the museum gallery from the half-landing below. The way they are gripped by two horizontal beams again shows how Mackintosh was influenced by Japanese methods of construction. The stair banisters rise to a rail that runs horizontally from the level of the highest step of each flight. Everything conspires to lead the eye onwards and upwards towards the museum above. The way light floods through the glass roof above and down into the stairwell only reinforces this sense of invitation.

### GLASGOW SCHOOL OF ART *1896–9*

## MUSEUM

*Courtesy of the Glasgow Picture Library*

IN the governors' brief for the competition, it was suggested that the museum might be 'a feature in connection with the staircase'. Certainly the way the staircase is constructed issues an invitation to follow it up into the light-filled museum. The glass roof provides light for the exhibits but also allows light to stream through to the staircase and the ground-floor corridor below. Mackintosh's fascination with Japanese construction techniques and design can be seen clearly in aspects of the museum's design: the way the uprights from the floor below are clasped between two horizontal beams, the timber truss work and the exposed rafters. The four posts of the staircase have what architectural historian Nikolaus Pevsner called 'mortarboard' cappings. Just for symmetry, Mackintosh adds two more caps on each of the outside trusses, but without the posts below. Originally he intended to use steel trusses in the roof, but he changed his mind and used timber instead. The central sections of the trusses have hearts carved in them in the manner of the great Arts and Crafts exponent Charles Voysey. Below them are the leaf shapes that characterise so much of Mackintosh's work. Both these touches add a playful note to a serious exhibition room.

## GLASGOW SCHOOL OF ART *1896–9*

# MACKINTOSH ROOM

*Courtesy of Mark Fiennes/Arcaid*

IN his original plans, Mackintosh created a magnificent unconventional boardroom in the east wing. Light flooded in through the pairs of bay windows at either end, where three panes of the windows allowed for ventilation, and the room was painted white to reflect all the available light. The curvature of the windows is accentuated by the timber in the bays themselves. Unfortunately, when Mackintosh made alterations between 1907 and 1909, he added an exterior staircase to the east wing which cuts past two of the windows, blocking the passage of light. By this time, though, the board of governors' dislike of the room and the fact that space was at such a premium meant that it was already being used as a studio. On the ceiling two reinforced-steel joists remain shamelessly exposed. The huge stone fireplace still dominates the room, the stone a reminder of the fabric of the building itself. The top of its wood surround meets the frieze rail that goes round the room at door height, lending the room a sense of enclosure. The hard angles of the fireplace and of the exposed joists are contrasted with the curved moulding of the fireplace, the semicircular inset above it and, of course, the window bays. A feature is made of the doors by framing them with tapering posts that join a projecting section of frieze rail. Each door has a triangular glass panel that contains a rooting seed head. Known today as the Mackintosh Room, it contains a collection of Mackintosh's furniture, though it is still used for committee meetings.

GLASGOW SCHOOL OF ART *1896–9*

# ROSE MOTIF IN DOORS OF STUDIO 45

*Courtesy of Eric Thorburn / Glasgow Picture Library*

ONE of Mackintosh's sources of inspiration was the book *Architecture, Mysticism and Myth* by the English architect, designer and teacher W. R. Lethaby. Here, Lethaby calls for a symbolic approach to architecture. Working with the Macdonald sisters, Mackintosh had already begun to develop his own organic imagery, which he was to use in much of his work. In the Glasgow School of Art, he lightened the severely utilitarian approach to the building with little touches that can be found in all sorts of places. Nearly every door has its own leaded-glass custodian in the form of an insect, seed or, as in the case of these doors to studio 45, rose. In his 1902 lecture 'Seemliness', Mackintosh propounded his ideas of the leaf as a symbol of life and the flower as a symbol of art: 'You must offer the flowers of the art that is in you – the symbol of all that is noble and beautiful and inspiring – flowers that will often change a colourless cheerless life into an animated thoughtful thing.' In his hands the rosebud became a highly charged symbol which he used particularly through the middle years of his career: from the entangled rose thickets in the Buchanan Street Tea Rooms, the Rose Boudoir in Turin and the Haus eines Kunstfreundes to the more abstract blooms on the walls of the Hill House, where they are absorbed into a more geometric design. The rose has been interpreted as representing Margaret's inspiration, the feminine round as opposed to the masculine square, signalling creativity, growth and love.

GLASGOW SCHOOL OF ART *1896–9*

## DECORATIVE TILES

*Courtesy of Eric Thorburn/Glasgow Picture Library*

THE walls of the Glasgow School of Art are punctuated by little flashes of colour which denote places of significance. Contrasting with the fragility of the organic motifs used by Mackintosh is the permanence of the square. The large square notice above the entrance to the school has smaller squares framing it, with four blocks of four-by-four squares giving a sense of solidity and strength. The east and west stairways are marked with combinations of green, white and blue tiles in different squared combinations. He punched square holes in doors, in the chairs in the director's room and, his most audacious use of the geometric combination, in the library lights. His use of the square did not begin and end here, but reappeared throughout his work. The Hill House (1902–4) provides a perfect example of how he blended the organic and geometric in a domestic setting. Everywhere, the square is dominant, whether in the carpet design, the chair-backs, the light fixtures or the wall stencilling. His fascination with the shape and its permutations is revealed more and more in his later work, from the chequered Dutch Kitchen in Miss Cranston's Argyle Street Tea Rooms and the latticework in the Chinese Room in the Ingram Street Tea Rooms to the extraordinary geometry-dependent rooms at 78 Derngate. The square provided a universal symbol of solidity and stability, its regular, right-angled sides a vital contrast to the fluidity of the organic imagery. More than that, it provided a shape with infinite possibilities for the sophisticated game-playing that Mackintosh enjoyed in much of his furniture design, including the cube table and the sixteen-legged clock he designed for the drawing room at the Hill House.

### GLASGOW SCHOOL OF ART 1907–9

## WEST FAÇADE

*Courtesy of Mark Fiennes / Arcaid*

TEN years after commissioning the first phase of the Glasgow School of Art, the board of governors decided it was time to complete the building. By now Mackintosh had developed and matured as an architect, as his redesign of the original plans for the west wing demonstrates. The largely blank return wall is built of the same rough stone as the east return wall, but here it acts as a foil for the smooth dressed stone of the rest of the façade. Three huge windows dominate the wall, soaring 25 feet upwards to light the library, their bays holding three of the windows of the floor below. Standing over a niche in the bay, each window is outlined by a rectilinear stone moulding enclosing a rough-hewn cylinder on either side of the glazing. These cylinders were to have been carved with decorative figures but budget constraints prevented it. Above them three horizontal windows contrast in size and movement, admitting light to the composition rooms. All the windows have the same nine-inch panes of glass, in direct contrast to the larger panes used on the north façade.

### GLASGOW SCHOOL OF ART *1907–9*

# DOOR OF WEST FAÇADE

*Courtesy of the Glasgow Picture Library*

THE door of the west façade is the building's most elaborate entrance. A low stone wall guides visitors in, its gently sculptured curves seducing them towards the doorway itself. The curves are repeated around the doorway but soon give way to the extraordinary angular architrave which adds an imposing grandeur of its own. It seems that Mackintosh enjoyed playing games as he pulled the frame forward while stepping back the wall behind. The effect, once again, is to draw visitors into the building. The removal of the upper part of the keystone is apparently a Mannerist conceit and a reminder of the niches in the window bays above. The stepped architrave around the upper part of the door foreshadows the work of the Art Deco movement. Mackintosh planned a carving above the architrave and possibly on the two cylinders either side of the door, but budget constraints meant they were never realised. As it was, the governors were furious that Mackintosh had ignored their demands for financial restraint in this second stage of building and committed them to what they considered an unnecessarily fanciful doorway.

GLASGOW SCHOOL OF ART *1907–8*

# WEST CORRIDOR

*Courtesy of the Glasgow Picture Library*

ON either side of the museum, corridors run east and west to give access to the antique and design rooms in the east and to the life rooms and library in the west. Casts are displayed along the west corridor, which is lit by three high windows where window seats can accommodate quiet meetings away from all the hurly-burly of the school. The corridors are particularly wide and the east one was used by students to work in until the second phase of building (1907–9) gave more space to the overcrowded school.

What makes the east corridor different from any other corridor in the school is the curiously shaped windows in the ceiling. This feature – which originally made it possible for students to work there – now means that the school's vast collection of casts can be effectively displayed. During the second building phase, runners were draped from the dark timber joists down the plaster wall, making it possible to hang casts there too. At that time, Mackintosh also added an exterior staircase at the end of the east corridor, which made access to the new upper floor a great deal more convenient, although unfortunately the staircase does have the disadvantage of blocking two of the windows looking out from the Mackintosh Room. The absence of doors in the corridor gives an uninterrupted view from one end of the school right the way through the museum to the other.

## GLASGOW SCHOOL OF ART *1907–9*

# LIBRARY

*Courtesy of Mark Fiennes / Arcaid*

THE library is commonly regarded as Mackintosh's tour de force within the School of Art. The room is divided by two rows of four wooden uprights that rest on the steel support beams below. The lower part of each upright consists of three sections, the central one extending up to the suspended ceiling, while the outer two carry the ends of the beams that run from the wall to support the balcony. To ensure that enough light reached the work spaces, the gallery was set back so that only the beams extend into the room. Above them the balustrades are chamfered and brightly painted with primary colours.

Mackintosh generally used more subtle pastel colours in his work, but these prefigure the more striking colours of his later work in the Dug Out in the basement of Miss Cranston's Willow Tea Rooms or in Mr Bassett-Lowke's 78 Derngate. The band of wood at the top of the balcony undulates gently round the room, catching the light on its curves and accommodating the gently rounded panels which resemble hanging banners. They reach below the balcony and end in varying abacus-like designs of small ovals carved in hanging columns.

The dominant straight lines of the timber posts and beams, of the coffered ceiling grid which in turn mirrors the window grid, are tempered by the curves found in the balcony and the chamfered banisters. The tall windows on the west side light the room, though they are cut both by the gallery and by the book store above (whose floor is the library's ceiling). The total effect has been compared to a grove of trees, light filtering through the sturdy timber uprights. The mood achieved is sombre and reflective, wholly conducive to study.

## GLASGOW SCHOOL OF ART *1907–9*

# LIBRARY: PERIODICALS TABLE

*Courtesy of David Churchill/Arcaid*

WHENEVER circumstances made it possible, Mackintosh took the trouble to design every aspect of the interiors of his buildings, including the furniture. Given his overview of rooms and buildings, it is little surprise that he wanted to ensure that all the constituent parts of his library were matching, of a whole.

The periodicals table, like so much else in the room, was especially designed by Mackintosh for use in the library. There is the hint of an interactive design element here. The lights suspended above the table (see page 66) appear to direct their light directly onto the table, ensuring a practical as well as decorative use of both. Made of stained cypress, the upper section that holds the magazines fits on to the top of the desk and is secured by clearly visible wedges at each end. The rack thus acts as both a practical receptacle for the newspapers and magazines for which it was designed and a physical barrier between the sides of the table. It ensures privacy while reading and adds to the air of quiet and an almost church-like austerity (the ends of the locking beams having almost a crucifix shape, the rack being almost spire-shaped). The design device of small oval shapes in uneven columns that features on the balcony panels is picked up and repeated here in the table legs and stretchers.

The other furniture that Mackintosh designed for the library included solid rectangular tables with crossed stretchers and the same abacus-like arrangement set into the legs, Windsor chairs (unfortunately these eventually proved too fragile for library use), a magazine stand and circular freestanding newspaper racks.

## GLASGOW SCHOOL OF ART *1907–9*

# LIBRARY: LIGHTS

*Courtesy of Mark Fiennes / Arcaid*

THE library is not a large room but Mackintosh manipulated the space to create a sense of openness and light. During the day, the room is largely lit by the floor-to-ceiling windows which extend up the west wall of the room. In winter, artificial light was obviously called for. The original brief for the school specified that the lighting should use the relatively modern source of electricity, giving Mackintosh new scope when it came to designing the light fittings. When electricity was first introduced, it was common to have the naked bulbs hanging unadorned, but Mackintosh seemed to revel in the opportunity to design another aspect of the room, using the shade to direct the light wherever he chose, illuminating specific areas and leaving others in shadow. It is pooled over the tables in the gallery and sides of the room, while the spectacular central light fitting illuminates the periodicals table below. Made up of thirteen suspended pierced-metal shades that are severely geometric in design, it resembles something from the New York skyline. Mackintosh succeeded in brilliantly exploiting the light so that it contributes to the overall sense of space in this expressive and dynamic interior.

## GLASGOW SCHOOL OF ART *1907–9*

# LIBRARY: INTERNAL WINDOWS

*Courtesy of Eric Thorburn / Glasgow Picture Library*

THE library in the Glasgow School of Art is not what it first appears. In fact, Mackintosh has used the original space to create three distinct areas: the library, the gallery and a hidden book store. The book store is concealed above the library space, and its floor forms the library's coffered ceiling. Mackintosh chose not to support the storeroom from below, but instead to hang it from steel brackets supported from its ceiling.

This imaginative choice gave him additional freedom when designing the library, because the timber posts do not have to do the work of supporting the ceiling. The floor of the store stops just before it meets the window. Here can be found another of Mackintosh's games, where he played the vertical (the window) off against the horizontal (the storeroom floor).

The interior plan is paramount and the exterior form does not necessarily reflect it. Seen from the outside, there are three massive windows, but inside Mackintosh draws first the balcony and then the ceiling across them. The radiators are placed by the windows, but if you lean over into the bay you can look up at the windows to the floor above. More extraordinary are the secondary inner windows that he designed in the inverted shape of the outer window, creating an internal glass tower. It is his obvious pleasure in such surprising conceits that makes many of Mackintosh's designs so infinitely rewarding.

GLASGOW SCHOOL OF ART *1907–9*

# LOGGIA

*Courtesy of Mark Fiennes / Arcaid*

BY 1907 Mackintosh had come up with the plans for the additional west wing of the School of Art and the necessary alterations to the existing building. At the south side of the building on the second floor he included a loggia which in his earlier plans had been a simple corridor. However, now the windows that had originally been planned to be flush with the building were bayed outwards and equipped with folding tables where the students could come to work or just stare thoughtfully out across the Glasgow rooftops. The solid brick arches make the room look oddly cellar-like – another of Mackintosh's visual jokes. When it was first used, the reddish brick walls were left bare, but at some later date it was decided to paint them white. Doing so may have lightened the space but it undoubtedly does away with the original character and leads to a rather chilly effect. The loggia runs behind the staff studios, linking the two composition rooms with the 'hen run' which eventually links with the embroidery room. At the east end of the loggia is a door that leads to the staircase spiralling up to the top of the east tower, from where there are sensational views across the city.

## GLASGOW SCHOOL OF ART *1907–9*

# THE 'HEN RUN'

*Courtesy of David Churchill / Arcaid*

UNLIKE the other three exterior walls, the south face of the Glasgow School of Art building is built of brick covered with harling (roughcast), which is strongly reminiscent of Scottish vernacular architecture and was a finish which Mackintosh used on both Windyhill and the Hill House.

Three wings extend back from the main body of the building in an E shape which is punctuated by windows only when absolutely necessary. The second phase of construction of the School of Art included the addition of the west wing, together with an external staircase to the east wing and an attic storey of studios at the top of the building. However, the existing director's studio blocked access between the first and second phases of building on the top floor. Mackintosh overcame this problem by creating the so-called 'hen run', a glass corridor that is cantilevered out behind the building and which connects the brick-arched loggia of the east wing and the corridor inset in the new west wing that leads through to the embroidery room.

The 'hen run' gained its odd name from the colloquial Glaswegian term 'hen', for a woman. Traditionally the sexes were segregated at the Glasgow School of Art, and the female students supposedly used this route to gain access to the male preserves on the other side.

## GLASGOW SCHOOL OF ART *1907–9*

## DIRECTOR'S OFFICE

*Courtesy of Mark Fiennes / Arcaid*

UNDER the directorship of Francis Newbery the Glasgow School of Art flourished and what became known as the Glasgow Style developed. Newbery's office is situated right at the front of the building, directly above the main entrance. It is particularly striking as one of Mackintosh's first white interiors. Up until this time the Victorians had preferred their rooms dark, white being used only for privies, sanatoriums and cowsheds. Mackintosh manipulates the space to divide it into two areas. By the asymmetrically placed window, the ceiling is lowered in an arch over the workspace. Newbery had his desk here, next to the hoist that delivered letters from the janitor's office on the floor below.

The larger area of the office was for discussion and has plenty of room for a large circular table and chairs. Running round the edge is a projecting cornice which gently follows the line of the arch down to where it meets the window top. Mackintosh panelled the room below the cornice, giving a certain intimacy. He included a generous amount of cupboard space and designed the imposing panelled fireplace as a central feature. Above this room is the director's studio, but the tight turn of the stair between them meant it was impossible to bring any large paintings down. The solution was a hole in the floor through which any size of canvas could be lowered. Mackintosh didn't design the furniture and lighting for here until 1904.

GLASGOW SCHOOL OF ART *1907–9*

# BOARDROOM

*Courtesy of Mark Fiennes / Arcaid*

WHEN Mackintosh designed the original boardroom in the east wing, it was airy, white and light, with pairs of bow windows at either end. But the members of the board were more used to the cramped, dark rooms of Victorian Scotland and felt decidedly ill at ease there. It wasn't until 1906 that the governors were rewarded with the sort of room they felt was more appropriate to their status and less unnervingly modern. The ground-floor studio on the east side of the entrance was adapted into something more fitting. This time Mackintosh created a formal room panelled in dark timber. Eight pilasters interrupt the panelling and are crowned with his idiosyncratic version of egg-and-dart moulding – an ironic nod to Classicism to tease the board members, half of whom were architects and many of whom he had fallen out with over his designs. The pilasters are fluted, thus allowing light to play on the wood. At the top, apparently random patterns are carved into the flutes which are reminiscent of the oval carvings on the balcony panels of the library. It has been suggested that they may represent musical notation. On the east wall, the panels cunningly disguise three doors to three presses. On the west is a door that opens into the office. The room is lit by three sets of nine lights that hang between the beams, each with a circular copper shade. New chairs were commissioned – solid-looking armchairs with three crescents cut out of their backs.

## MISS CRANSTON'S ARGYLE STREET TEA ROOMS, 114 ARGYLE STREET, GLASGOW *1897–9, 1906*

### LUNCHEON ROOM 1897

*Courtesy of the Hunterian Art Gallery,
University of Glasgow*

MISS Cranston's empire was growing – her tea rooms proved a safe haven in a city known to be in thrall to the demon drink. Middle-class men could meet there, but more importantly so could women who might feel threatened or whose reputation might be compromised if they were seen meeting in public houses. Here they could eat, drink tea and chat to their hearts' content. Mackintosh had already been involved in the decoration of the Buchanan Street Tea Rooms, working with George Walton. Now Miss Cranston was planning the enlargement of her Argyle Street premises and wanted their involvement again. However, this time their roles were reversed. It was Walton who designed and supervised the stencilled wall decorations, while Mackintosh designed the furniture. He used stained or varnished oak, largely in the tradition of the Arts and Crafts movement. The pieces were solid and functional, with an emphasis on square, box-like shapes. It was the work he did here that established his style for the next few years, until he and Margaret Macdonald married and moved into their flat at 120 Mains Street.

## MISS CRANSTON'S ARGYLE STREET TEA ROOMS *1897–9, 1906*

# HIGH-BACKED OAK CHAIR

*Courtesy of the Hunterian Art Gallery, University of Glasgow*

WHEN Mackintosh and George Walton were employed by Miss Cranston to design her enlarged and redecorated Argyle Street Tea Rooms, Mackintosh made full use of the commission to establish his own style. This high-backed chair, the first of many that he designed, is a fine example.

Made of stained oak, the chair's legs are rectangular at the foot, becoming in turn oval and then circular at the top. The oval back panel, with its cutout of a stylised bird in flight, slots into the legs, while the wide, flat uprights lightly skim the back of the seat before joining on to the base of the design.

The chair's high back was intended to give a sense of privacy and enclosure to people sitting around a table sipping tea and it also served spatially to divide the tea room into small, apparently self-contained areas. Although Mackintosh designed the chair with this function much in mind, the high back was a feature that he was to develop and play with continually until it became one of the best-recognised elements of his work.

Mackintosh was in fact particularly pleased with this design and he used it again both in his own homes and in his drawings for the competition for Haus eines Kunstfreundes in 1901.

## MISS CRANSTON'S
## ARGYLE STREET TEA ROOMS *1897–9, 1906*

## DESIGN FOR A HATSTAND

*Courtesy of the Hunterian Art Gallery,*
*University of Glasgow*

MACKINTOSH'S drawing for a hatstand epitomises the simplicity of design he chose to use in the Argyle Street Tea Rooms. It is an extremely basic construction of four planks, subtly curved at the foot, rising to come together under a wooden crown. A row of six metal hooks at the top is balanced by a further row of four below. The base of each upright is flanked by two drip-trays to catch the water from the umbrellas held by the attractively twisted metal holders above. This style of furniture has been dubbed Mackintosh's 'plank style'. It gives the furniture a solid and perhaps surprisingly masculine feel which is similar to the furniture being produced by the Arts and Crafts movement. Mackintosh took care to relieve the solid rectangular shapes with judiciously placed curves, carvings or cutouts. Of course, the tea rooms were not meant just as retreats for women but were extended to include smoking and billiards rooms and men's lunch rooms too. However, the unusually bold furniture was not designed exclusively for use by men by any means: the sturdiest chairs were to be found in the ladies' reading room.

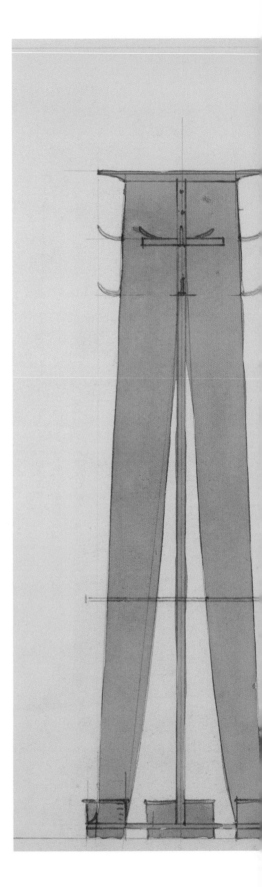

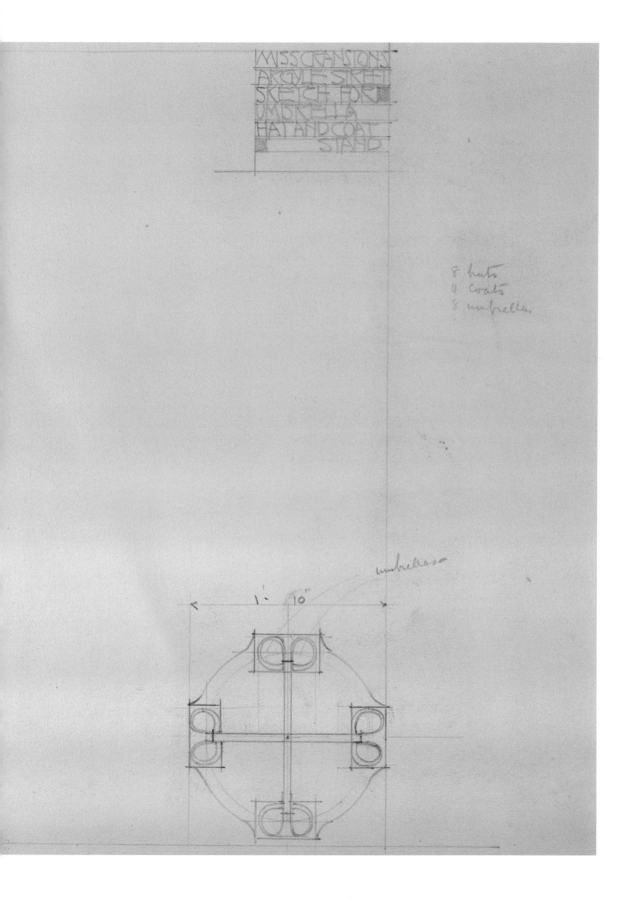

## MISS CRANSTON'S
## ARGYLE STREET TEA ROOMS *1897–9, 1906*

# DUTCH KITCHEN

*Courtesy of T. & R. Annan & Sons*

TEN years after designing the furniture for the Argyle Street Tea Rooms, Mackintosh was asked by Miss Cranston to create the Dutch Kitchen in the basement of the premises. By this time George Walton had left Glasgow, so the job was entirely Mackintosh's. He took quite a different approach from the one used in the rooms above. Developing the theme he had begun at the Hill House, he used the square as his main motif. He drove the workmen to distraction insisting that they lay the black-and-white-chequered lino at right angles to the wall, not on the usual diagonal. In the inglenook, the checks were reduced to half-size with dazzling effect, while vertical and horizontal bands of checks ran down the central columns of the room, along the dado rail and even on the dresser. The severity of the geometry was relieved by the curved design of the chairs and the arch of the ingle, which mirrors the curve of the fireplace, while the grate curved gently into the wall and the hearth bowed slightly outwards. The room was painted entirely in black and white; no allowances were to be made for the fact that this is a dingy basement with little light. The only colour introduced was the brilliant emerald green of the chairs.

# QUEEN'S CROSS CHURCH, GARSCUBE ROAD, GLASGOW *1898*

## VIEW FROM THE SOUTH-WEST

*Courtesy of Eric Thorburn / Glasgow Picture Library*

IT is thought that Mackintosh began work on the design of Queen's Cross Church shortly after he had completed his competition entry for the Glasgow School of Art in 1896. But probably because of the problems presented by the awkward corner site, the first foundation stone was not laid for two years. This is the only church Mackintosh designed that was realised, although he did contribute to the internal design of Holy Trinity, Bridge of Allen and Abbey Close Church, Paisley, not to mention his submission to a competition for the Liverpool Anglican Cathedral in 1903 for which he was highly commended. His ingenious solutions to the problem plot and ways of access are noteworthy. His brief demanded a galleried church to seat around seven hundred people, plus a hall that was linked to both the church and the street. Mackintosh took the focus of the site, the corner, and made the most of it with the oversized tower which, in comparison with the rest of the building, is bulky but imposing. It is thought that his inspiration came from a parish church in Merriot, Somerset. He took the traditional element – the main entrance in the tower, usually at the rear of the nave – and brought it to the front of the building beside the altar, allowing access to the aisle on the street side which also leads to two stairs up to the balconies. The building has been the headquarters of the Charles Rennie Mackintosh Society since 1977.

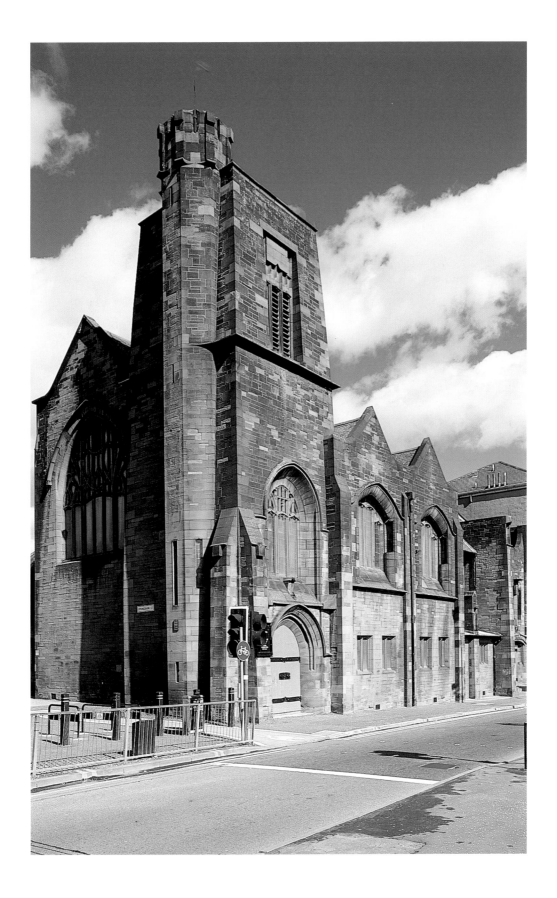

## QUEEN'S CROSS CHURCH *1898*

# DETAIL OVER THE EAST PORCH

*Courtesy of Eric Thorburn / Glasgow Picture Library*

THE dour treatment of the Queen's Cross Church façade allowed Mackintosh to relieve it with the playfulness of discreet ornamental carvings which are Art Nouveau in character. Inside the church as well, the carving on the capitals of the nave pillars derives from the same source.

Like the Mannerists, Mackintosh sometimes used the traditional elements of architecture only to exaggerate them, distorting their proportions until they transcended their origins and became something new. In this case, the oversized mullion above the east porch stretches above and below the limits of the window, with ornamental carving at either end. This fanciful treatment is reinforced by the play of the glass, stone and light, which results in the stone seeming almost to be the more delicate and malleable material.

Mackintosh's supreme eye for detail makes Queen's Cross Church an extraordinary treasure trove of different subtleties: flying buttresses, an interrupted roofline, varied window designs and, of course, the stumpy tower with the stair turret rising from it. He employed Gothic elements in the design both inside and outside the building, but rejected any sense of the order that would normally be imposed on them. Instead he massed the elements together just in the way that Free Style architects were beginning to do in domestic architecture – an area into which he was about to move.

QUEEN'S CROSS CHURCH *1898*

## DETAIL OF CARVED PANELS OF THE PULPIT

*Courtesy of Eric Thorburn / Glasgow Picture Library*

THE interior of the church is surprisingly light and spacious given its cramped appearance from the outside. The chancel window is set slightly off centre to accommodate the vestry and session house above. The two galleries are cantilevered out beyond their supporting pillars in a way favoured by the Japanese. Another debt to Japanese building techniques is seen in the construction and carving of the roof trusses, which echo those in the museum at the Glasgow School of Art. As with the exterior, it is the detailing that is so remarkable. The carving on the wall panelling, the pulpit, the communion table and the stonework of the pillars all use the private organic symbolism of the Four. The pulpit shows stylised birds' heads and leaves, while at the back of the pulpit the oval panel is a reminder of the oval-backed chairs designed for the Argyle Street Tea Rooms.

On the balcony fronts in particular, the abstraction of the organic forms foreshadows those used by Mackintosh in the library of the Glasgow School of Art. He achieved wonders in such a limited space largely by his use of a vaulted timber ceiling and unashamed exposure of the reinforced riveted steel joists. This is effectively a medieval construction using modern materials and is thought to have been inspired by the Gothic Revival Church of the Holy Trinity, Latimer Road, London, which was designed a decade earlier using the same exposed tie beams across the arched ceiling.

# RUCHILL STREET FREE CHURCH HALLS, RUCHILL STREET, GLASGOW *1898–9*

## FAÇADE

*Courtesy of David Churchill/Arcaid*

THIS is considered by many to be a minor work but is none the less visually pleasing. The brief was to provide two halls, a committee room, a store, offices and lavatories. This Mackintosh did by having the hall, store and committee room on the ground floor. The upper floor was reached by a picturesque stair tower in traditional Scottish vernacular style, with a conical roof, at the rear of the building. Upstairs is another hall, committee room, store and lavatories. Economically planned, the rooms work well individually and can also be enlarged by moving partitions or opening wide doors so they run together. Mackintosh was again demonstrating how he could manipulate space. The internal doors do feature some stained-glass work but he seems not to have designed any furniture. The rear of the building is finished in harling (roughcast) but the front is of solid grey sandstone. Here he used his talent to enliven a building where the brief and the accommodation did not strictly justify any individual treatment. He animated a straightforward façade by using standard architectural features of the time – the four-bayed ground-floor window, the corbels and the curved pediment – but putting them together to create the illusion of a face. All the more appropriate that the mouth should be for the larger hall, where a small crowd could be addressed. Incidentally, it is believed that Mackintosh had the opportunity to design the adjoining church but lost the job because of the difficult way he behaved over his handling of the church halls' commission.

# WESTDEL, 2 QUEEN'S PLACE, DOWANHILL, GLASGOW *c.1898*

## BEDROOM: SOUTH WALL ELEVATION

*Courtesy of the Hunterian Art Gallery,
University of Glasgow*

WESTDEL was the Glasgow home of Robert Maclehose, a discerning publisher and bookseller. He commissioned Mackintosh to design a second-floor bedroom and adjoining bathroom.

Mackintosh produced three pencil and watercolour elevations for the bedroom that showed the exact interrelationship between the different elements. The drawings themselves were unusual because rather than being standard architect's plans, they were works of art in their own right, one of them being exhibited at the Glasgow Institute of Fine Arts exhibition in 1899. The room itself was remarkable because it was one of the first of Mackintosh's white rooms. Other architects and designers had used white in bedrooms and even white furniture, but Mackintosh was the first to create such a unified whole. Quite how much involvement Margaret Macdonald had in the scheme is unknown but it is thought that her influence can be seen in the decorative touches. A frieze rail ran round the room at door height. Below it, timber uprights divided the wall into sections, while above it ran a stencilled frieze. The drawing shows how the furniture was designed to fit exactly into the scheme. Mackintosh's organic imagery also served to unify the whole: the roses and flower heads were joined by delicate fluid carving of a tree on the foot of the bed and a glorious peacock stencil over the fireplace. Straight lines were complemented by the subtle use of curves in the bed ends, the fireplace and the mouldings.

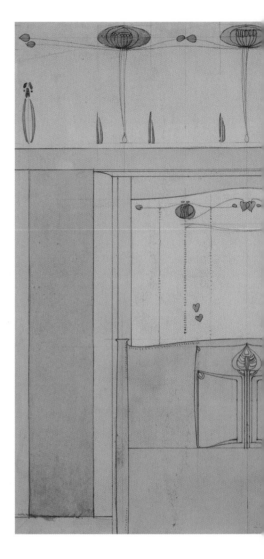

# 120 MAINS STREET, GLASGOW *1900*

## STUDIO DRAWING ROOM

*Courtesy of the Hunterian Art Gallery, University of Glasgow*

THE Mackintoshes moved into 120 Mains Street in 1900, just after they were married, and lived there until they moved to 6 Florentine Terrace in 1906. This marked a turning point in Mackintosh's domestic work as they completely refurbished the flat, working with light, colour and symbolism in a way that was totally unique at the time. Finally they had the opportunity to put their design theories into practice. In *Das Englische Haus* (1904) Herman Muthesius wrote, 'Mackintosh's interiors achieve a level of sophistication that is way beyond the lives of even the artistically educated section of the population.' The house was Victorian and the rooms had typically grand dimensions. In the drawing room the couple created a more intimate sense by using a frieze rail around the room, continuing it across the windows to bring unity to the scheme, breaking it only by oval cutouts through which the window catch could be reached. The walls were divided at intervals by using uprights which ended in a fin on the frieze rail, flanked by two squares. The panels that were left between them were covered in grey canvas. All the furniture was painted white, as were the windows frames, skirting board, frieze and ceiling. The grand fireplace was made of wood and played a dominant role in the room, designed to the last inch, even including space for two cushions for their two grey cats. Against the other walls were a long, low bookcase with elegant stained-glass and leaded windows and a heavy writing desk which incorporated beaten-metal designs by Margaret. Everything was self-consciously positioned in the room, down to the high-backed chair that stood between the two windows. Lighting was another important consideration. The daylight filtered through fine muslin curtains, while at night strategically hung gas lamps in groups of four provided a soft light in the room. Unlike traditionally overcrowded Victorian rooms, this was a hymn to a new minimalism.

**120 MAINS STREET** *1900*

## DINING ROOM

*Courtesy of the Hunterian Art Gallery, University of Glasgow*

THIS was the only room in the Mackintoshes' flat at Mains Street not to receive the white treatment. Being a flat and in winter particularly in need of as much light as possible (the days begin late and end early), finding the sombre interior of the dining room is almost a shock. However, in late-nineteenth-century Scotland one might have expected a smaller room like this to be decorated in a subdued way. Eating was a serious business and should be done in a more sombre, masculine atmosphere (the man did, after all, provide whatever means there were in the household and they were often very hard-won). In this room attention could be properly focused not on the decoration, but on what was on the table.

As had been done in the drawing room, the walls were divided by a wooden frieze rail, which was this time stained dark and aligned with the top of the door. Above the rail everything was painted white, but below it the walls were covered with brown wrapping paper which was stencilled.

All the furniture in the room was made of stained oak and was kept extremely simple. The dining table was plain and rectangular, but subtly ornamented with two double flower petals on either side. The fireplace in the dining room was far less intrusive than that in the drawing room by virtue of its being painted black. In any event, making a statement with it would have been difficult, given its position in a corner of the room. The room was lit by candles on wall sconces which were attached to two tapering posts.

**120 MAINS STREET** *1900*

# BEDROOM

*Courtesy of the Glasgow Picture Library*

ALTHOUGH the Mackintoshes' bedroom at Mains Street was smaller than any of the other rooms in the flat, furniture was nevertheless crammed into it.

The first white bedroom that Mackintosh designed, for the publisher Robert Maclehose at Westdel, anticipated his treatment of his own bedroom here. The walls and ceiling were painted white and so too was the furniture. By using white paint, Mackintosh was able to explore a radically new kind of furniture design and, more advantageously perhaps, he was able also to cover over the obvious structural details of the pieces. Obviously the white furniture would reflect what natural light was available and, as far as possible, give an impression of the room being bigger than it was. It's difficult to underestimate how radical the use of white was here. Standard, Victorian and Victorian-inspired furniture was large, usually dark (although occasionally walnut), and ornate. The wardrobes here are as big as the standard fare, and carry as much adornment, yet they appear radically different.

A massive double wardrobe stood against one wall, with high-relief carvings of birds on its doors. (The doors may originally have been decorated with inlaid glass or coloured paint.) The stylised organic shape of its handles was repeated on the sides of the cheval mirror and on the foot of the bed. These curves contrasted with and complement the straight lines throughout the rest of the room.

The bed itself was a large yet intimate four-poster, curtained to keep out the draughts, and the coloured organic designs stencilled on to the frieze rail were repeated on the embroidered bedlinen and the valance.

## WINDYHILL, KILMACOLM, RENFREWSHIRE *1900–1*

### VIEW FROM THE NORTH-EAST

*Courtesy of Eric Thorburn / Glasgow Picture Library*

IT is thought that Francis Newbery, director of the Glasgow School of Art, introduced Mackintosh to the Davidson family. Between 1894 and 1897, Mackintosh designed various pieces of furniture for their Gladsmuir home. Windyhill was subsequently commissioned by William Davidson Jr for his young family. This was Mackintosh's first opportunity to design both the interior and the exterior of a house and it is reasonable to assume that he followed his habit of letting the all-important interior plan dictate the exterior appearance. Perched on the summit of a hill in Kilmacolm, facing south-west towards Duchal Moor, it commands magnificent views. Mackintosh employed the traditional design of an L shape, the long arm of the L containing a ground-floor hall off which opened the dining room, living room and playroom, with a corridor and bedrooms upstairs. The short arm contained the service wing and accommodation for the servants. The house is approached from the north, with the lower-roofed service wing on the east. On the outside, he used a Free Style reworking of such traditional features as the pitched roofs, gable ends and wide chimneys. The whole building was finished in grey harling (roughcast), which had been common to Scottish architecture for centuries. However, Mackintosh went one step further and took the harling right up to the window edges, so the emphasis of the building is on the way its different forms mass together, not on the individual components.

# WINDYHILL *1900–1*

## BOOKCASE IN THE DRAWING ROOM

*Courtesy of Eric Thorburn / Glasgow Picture Library*

DAVIDSON brought some furniture with him from his family home, so Mackintosh was limited in the pieces that he could design. His principal contributions were in the living room, hall, playroom and master bedroom. He chose to use stained and polished oak for all the pieces, except those in the bedroom, which were painted white. The dining room was panelled throughout, giving a typically sombre surround for the business of eating and drinking. From photographs of the time, the living room seems to have been painted the same pale shade from floor to ceiling, except for the west wall, which carried a dark paper up to a frieze rail. It was against this wall that the magnificent bookcase stood. Like the rest of the furniture Mackintosh designed for the house, it was made in a simple plank style but was embellished with his trademark features. The base shelves are apparently flanked by solid columns. However, turn them to the side and more shelves are revealed.

The top part consists of two cabinets on either side of a void, giving the piece a kimono shape. Mackintosh relieved the solid squared-off appearance by adding leaded glass panels and introducing the subtle curves in the top of the lower section that are anchored by the bud-like carving. Similarly, above the void, a cap with carving breaks the line and centres the piece.

## WINDYHILL *1900–1*

# LIGHT FITTING OVER THE STAIRS

*Courtesy of Eric Thorburn / Glasgow Picture Library*

THE hall at Windyhill was a long, wide, north-facing room that could be used for large family parties. Mackintosh decorated it austerely, leaving the dark-stained joists exposed in the ceiling but keeping the walls white, in contrast with the dark wood skirting, frieze rail and doors. He framed the fireplace in wood with two squared uprights that narrowed towards their own cornice above. The room was furnished with stained oak furniture made in the sturdy plank style. The west end of the hall led to the stair bay, which rose to the upper corridor. The curved stairway was lit by tall narrow windows, anticipating a style commonly used twenty years later. Above it hung this splendidly idiosyncratic light which has unmistakable Mackintosh hallmarks. At this time Windyhill would have had only gas lighting, so light fixtures had to be open for air and fumes to pass through. In the hall itself the shades were kept relatively simple, using glass squares, but in the stairway Mackintosh allowed himself something more elaborate. The metal frame was punctured with small squares at the top, echoing those in the hall, and with abstract flower heads. The light shone softly through the panes of pink glass, warming the walls. A circular band around the base carried eight candles to add to the mood, while from the top hung little glass ornaments.

# DAILY RECORD BUILDING,
# RENFREW LANE, GLASGOW *1900–4*

## FAÇADE

*Courtesy of Eric Thorburn / Glasgow Picture Library*

THE site for the *Daily Record*'s offices was long and rectangular, facing out into Renfrew Lane, a particularly narrow street. In other public and commercial buildings, Mackintosh used glazing as a key element in the variation of the façade. Here, following the Free Style approach, he used the masonry to create dramatic contrast and variety on the left side of the building, which had its upper storeys added in 1903 and 1904. At ground level, the stonemasonry is reminiscent of Egyptian or Inca walls in its monumental dimensions, with everything suggesting weight and mass, although in seeming contradiction the arches above the windows look almost too shallow for the weight they are carrying, the doorway too narrow for the immense keystone crowning it. However, as soon as the eye reaches the upper floors, the vocabulary changes and a much more delicate treatment of wall and openings suits the increased available light.

Unusually for Mackintosh, there is a dramatic change of scale between the treatment of the ground floor, the main body of the building and the roof, which exhibits a traditional Renaissance approach. In the dormer windows, he reversed the rhythm of the arches below to cap the façade, again accentuating the theme of the keystone in the dormer windows, exaggerating it as an ornament. Here too are echoes of the Scottish baronial style of architecture he used to such effect on the Glasgow Herald Building.

## DAILY RECORD BUILDING *1900–4*

# DETAIL OF THE FAÇADE

*Courtesy of Eric Thorburn / Glasgow Picture Library*

MACKINTOSH chose to use glazed bricks to clad the front of the Daily Record Building. Glazed bricks were common in gloomy Victorian light wells because they reflected light back into the building, but their purpose here was different. The site on which he had to work was unusually dark, even for Glasgow. There may well be a slight conceit in the use of such light-reflecting material to adorn the offices of a newspaper, too.

Apart from purely practical considerations of durability, Mackintosh must have liked the contrast between the machine-produced smoothness and skin-like sheen of the bricks' enamel surface and the stark roughness of the masonry above and below. This masculine–feminine dynamic is further emphasised by Mackintosh's playful use of green and red glazed tiles to create patterns and enrich the otherwise severe continuity of the façade. The green glazed tiles reach upwards at intervals towards the roof until they meet the triangular design in red tiles that symbolically reproduces a favoured motif, that of the tree of life, similar to the one used on the Passmore Edwards Settlement in London.

The light-hearted and unashamed use of external decoration here gives an almost Viennese character to the façade, which is in sharp contrast with the rest of Mackintosh's rather more austere building design. The use of tree shapes among the brick and tiles of what is a predominantly industrial area, albeit one of offices rather than factories, suggests Mackintosh's longing for natural elements in the middle of the city. In a way they are strangely reminiscent of the great Catalan architect Antonio Gaudí's use of natural shapes, constructed of man-made materials, which adorn, support and intrude upon his exotic work.

## MISS CRANSTON'S INGRAM STREET TEA ROOMS, GLASGOW *1900, 1907, 1909, 1910–11*

### WASSAIL

*Courtesy of the Hunterian Art Gallery, University of Glasgow*

MISS Cranston was continuing to expand her business fast. By 1900 she had acquired two new shops (numbers 213 and 215) to add to the tea room and luncheon room she had already established in Ingram Street. Mackintosh and Margaret were commissioned to design the interiors together. This was the first time Mackintosh was to have a free hand in the overall design of a tea room, and he rose to the challenge. He and Margaret had just finished redecorating 120 Mains Street and they used the same principles for the first time in a public space, creating a stylised domesticity. He admitted as much light as possible into the ground-floor ladies' luncheon room by introducing veiled full-height windows onto the street. The room was subdivided by wooden screens that echoed the silver-painted panelling around the room. Above the frieze on either side of the room were fine gesso panels: *The Wassail* by Mackintosh and *The May Queen* by Margaret, both with overtones of pagan festivities that celebrated the changing of the seasons. They were constructed on large pieces of hessian, using coloured plaster as a background, string to define the figures and coloured beads and glass for decoration. The groups of women depicted were clearly in the style of the Four and because the panels had no title on display, the customers would have been ignorant of their significance – just aware of the mysterious women looking down over them.

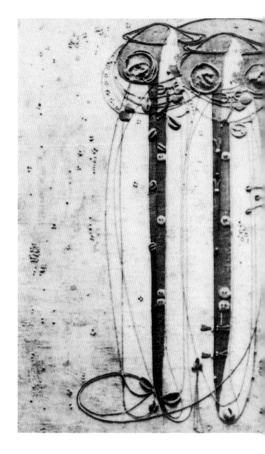

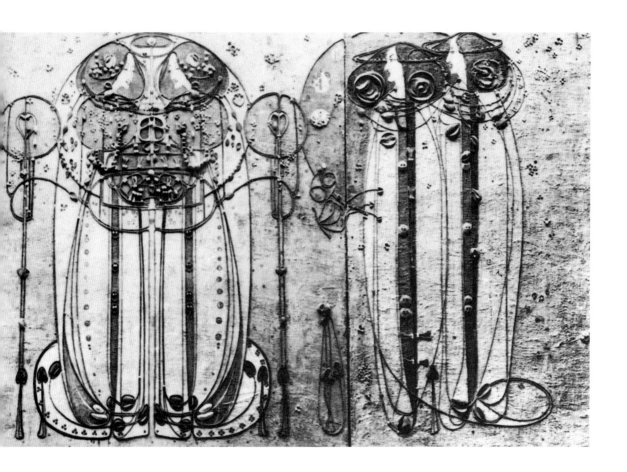

## MISS CRANSTON'S INGRAM STREET TEA ROOMS

# CHINESE ROOM

*Courtesy of the Hunterian Art Gallery,
University of Glasgow*

IN 1911 Miss Cranston asked Mackintosh to redesign the men's tea room in her Ingram Street premises. This was to mark a significant change in his work. The style of the day favoured Moorish or oriental detail in places where men gathered for refreshment or to be entertained. Accordingly, Mackintosh created the Chinese Room as a spectacular work of fantasy combined with his obsession with squares. The walls were lined with canvas protected by latticework and the space enclosed and roofed by a latticework structure. All of this was painted brilliant blue under a black ceiling. Pagoda-shaped structures were placed on top of the roof and similar shapes hung down with the lightshades beneath. The severe rectilinear design was relieved by the extraordinary door canopy, the pay desk and the concave pieces of glass or the new plastic that filled the latticework projecting from the wall. All the fittings were painted in blue, red or black, a radical departure from the more subdued spots of colour used in his earlier work. Exploiting the contrasts between light and dark, open and shut, square and fluid, Mackintosh created a complex and spectacular room.

## Miss Cranston's
## Ingram Street Tea Rooms

# Chairs and domino table

*Courtesy of the Glasgow Picture Library*

THE tea rooms were not only for eating and drinking, but were places where men could come to smoke and play billiards or cards. The already large premises of Ingram Street had been further expanded when Miss Cranston bought number 217 in 1907. Mackintosh was commissioned to create the galleried Oak Room. It was long and narrow with a gallery along three sides.

The commission came at a time when he was beginning to get less work, though he was kept painfully busy with the Glasgow School of Art. In fact, the Oak Room had similarities with the school's library: both had a gallery and the curves of the library's chamfered balustrades are seen again in the wavy lines Mackintosh used as decoration and in some of the chair-backs. He had earlier designed similar domino tables for the Argyle Street Tea Rooms, but without these comfortable bucket chairs neatly repeating the shape of the table.

## 14 KINGSBOROUGH GARDENS, GLASGOW *1901–2*

### DRAWING ROOM

*Courtesy of the Hunterian Art Gallery,*
*University of Glasgow*

TOWARDS the end of 1901 Mrs Rowat, the mother-in-law of Francis Newbery, director of the Glasgow School of Art, commissioned Mackintosh to decorate several rooms and remodel the dining-room fireplace of her terraced house in Glasgow's West End. The work was completed in two stages, the freestanding furniture being commissioned after the walls and fitted pieces were complete. Again, the evident femininity in the decor suggests the influence of Margaret. As with his designs for Mains Street, Mackintosh left the Victorian cornice intact and brought the eyeline down by running a door-high frieze rail around the room. Instead of the stark austerity of the bare walls at his home, Mrs Rowat's walls were alive with delicately stencilled mauve and grey roses. The backs of the seats also had a repeated stencil design. Such intense and busy patterning comes as a surprise after the more restrained drawing rooms Mackintosh had designed both for himself and for William Davidson's Windyhill. Contrasted with the natural forms is the firmly geometric fireplace made of painted wood with a square grate and decorative inlaid-glass shapes, though it didn't escape the addition of three buds. A favourite piece of Mackintosh's was the oval table which he had made for his own use. The high-backed chairs with rich purple velvet upholstery look surprisingly flimsy after the more solid furniture he had been designing for Miss Cranston's tea rooms.

## 14 KINGSBOROUGH GARDENS *1901–2*

# WHITE CABINET

*Courtesy of the Glasgow Picture Library*

THIS cabinet was originally made for Mrs Rowat when Mackintosh carried out internal renovations at 14 Kingsborough Gardens. He also had one made for his own drawing room at 120 Mains Street. At first glance a simple white-painted oak cabinet, the doors open to reveal silvered insides inlaid with coloured glass. The glass image depicts one of the attenuated women so popular with the Four holding a flowering rose and is thought to have been designed by Margaret.

The exquisite precision of the design meant that the cabinet was often kept open to display the interior. The organic symbolism present in the rest of the room is repeated with the three rosebuds adorning the ends of the shelf divides. The femininity of the piece is enhanced by the introduction of slight curves to the lower edge and corner of the door and to the central divider and top shelf. The sides of the lower section of the cabinet have a central fin which gently tapers towards the top, culminating in a simple, oddly ocular carving.

This piece is a true and original triumph of design and sophistication.

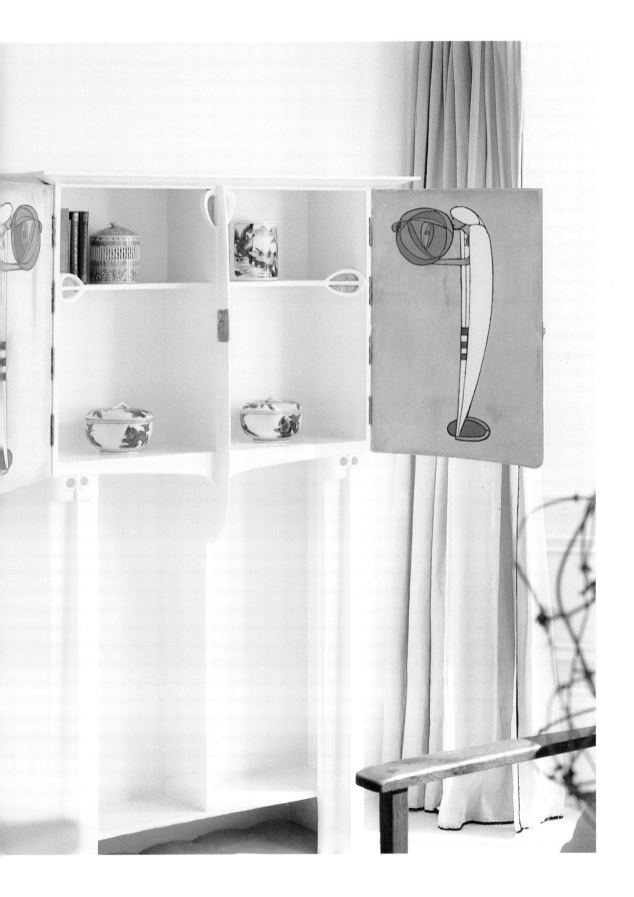

# Haus Eines Kunstfreundes (House for an Art Lover) *1901*

## Exterior elevation for competition

*Courtesy of the Hunterian Art Gallery,*
*University of Glasgow*

IN 1901 the magazine *Zeitschrift für Innendekoration* announced a competition for the design, both exterior and interior, and decoration for a large country house for a connoisseur of the arts. Mackintosh entered his plans for a building he called Der Vogel (The Bird) but was disqualified on the grounds that he failed to submit the required number of interior designs. However, when the designs were eventually complete, he was awarded a special prize of 600 marks. The prize itself was not awarded, but his designs and those of the winner of the second prize, fellow Scot Hugh Baillie Scott, and the winner of the third prize, Leopold Bauer, were considered the best entries and they were subsequently published by Alexander Koch, whose brainchild the competition was. They appeared in portfolio form under the title 'Meister der Innenkunst' (Masters of Interior Design).

Mackintosh's house took some of the ideas he had used in his designs for Windyhill. The house had a white harling (roughcast) finish, its appearance defined by the massing of shapes and the dominance of broad unadorned planes. The positioning of the windows depended on the interior plan, not on any formal requirements of the exterior design. The result was unconventional and original.

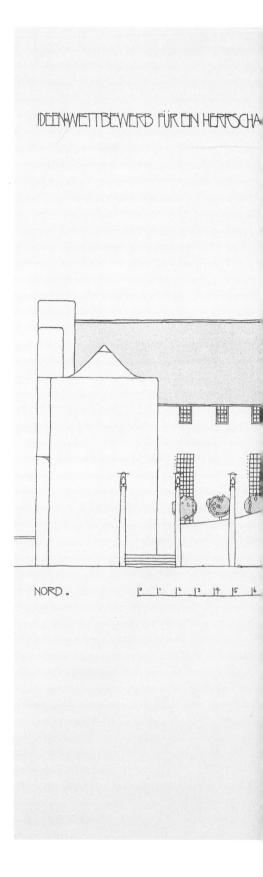

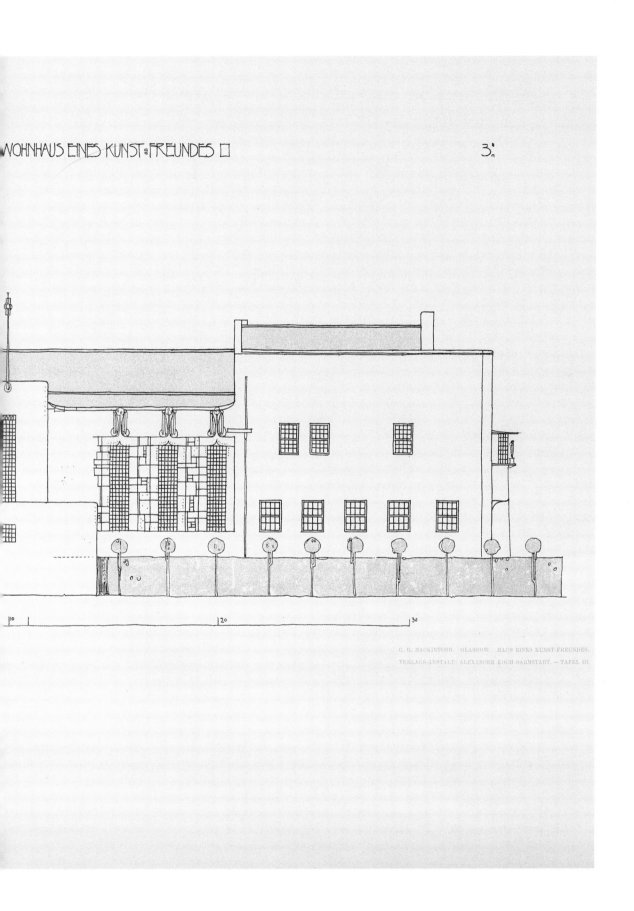

WOHNHAUS EINES KUNST·FREUNDES ☐

3.

C. R. MACKINTOSH, GLASGOW. — HAUS EINES KUNST-FREUNDES.
VERLAGS-ANSTALT: ALEXANDER KOCH-DARMSTADT. — TAFEL III

## HAUS EINES KUNSTFREUNDES *1901*

## FLOOR PLANS FOR THE FIRST AND SECOND FLOORS

*Courtesy of the Hunterian Art Gallery,*
*University of Glasgow*

THERE is no doubt that Mackintosh worked closely with Margaret on the plans for the Haus Eines Kunstfreundes. The interiors followed the same pattern he employed at Mains Street, culminating in his work at the Hill House: the masculine/feminine coding, the planned movement from exterior to interior, the contrast of dark with light. The entrance was on the north side of the building by the courtyard, up some steps and into an enclosed porch which opened into a long east–west galleried corridor and hall. The dining room opened off the north-west side of the hall, separated only by a partition which can be removed when required.

The principal rooms of the house were all south-facing, allowing the sun to provide maximum light and warmth during the day. Next to the study was the impressive oval room or ladies' sitting room, but the pièce de résistance was the huge drawing room and music room. They could be used separately or combined into one magnificent space with wide doors to the hall. Upstairs the main bedrooms opened off the corridor and gallery on to the south-facing side of the house, giving views across the garden. The children's, nurse's and breakfast rooms all occupied the west end of the floor, with a playroom wisely in the attic above.

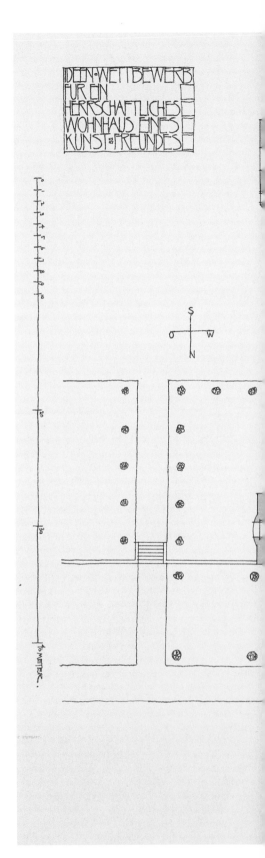

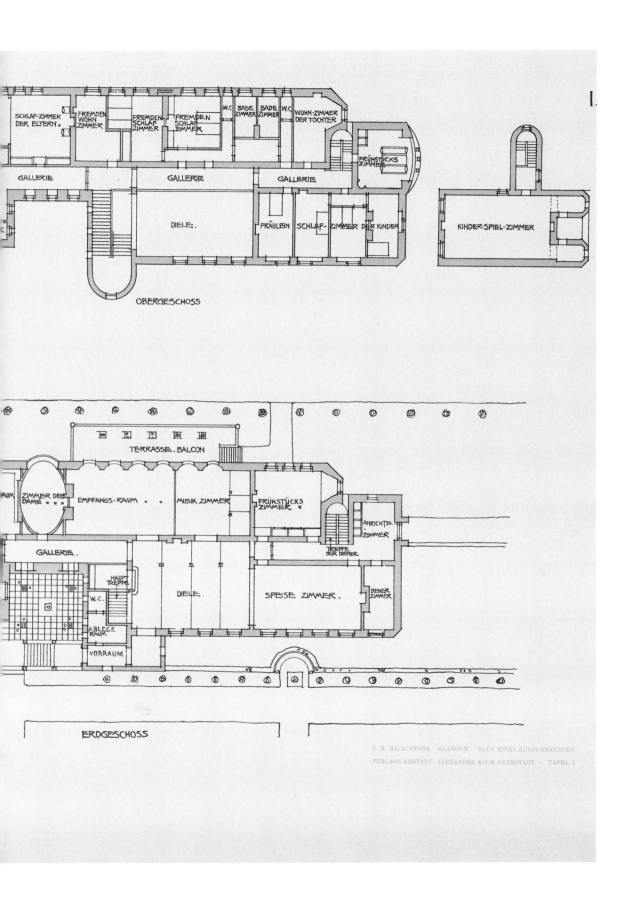

OBERGESCHOSS

ERDGESCHOSS

C. R. MACKINTOSH, GLASGOW. HAUS EINES KUNST-FREUNDES.
VERLAGS-ANSTALT: ALEXANDER KOCH-DARMSTADT. — TAFEL I.

### HAUS EINES KUNSTFREUNDES *1901*

## DESIGN FOR
## SOUTH WALL OF THE HALL

*Courtesy of the Hunterian Art Gallery,*
*University of Glasgow*

THE hall was a typically subdued room providing
the halfway point between the outside world and the
private rooms that lead off it. Sturdy timber columns
supported the gallery upstairs, which had a solid
balustrade cut with ellipses at the lower edge which
were mirrored in the shape of the fireplace hood and
the convex curves of the upper section. The pendants
on the balustrade were a device that Mackintosh
used earlier in Queen's Cross Church.

The columns were reminiscent of those used in
the library of the Glasgow School of Art, except here
the narrow column on the upper floor appeared to
rise from the centred section of the lower column.
The lower supports provided a grid into which were
fitted the fireplace and the doors to the reception
room. The dark and imposing solid timber was
lightened by the decorated panelling on the uprights
and fireplace, while light came through the leaded
and stained-glass windows in the door of the
reception room, inviting visitors in and hinting at the
marvels beyond.

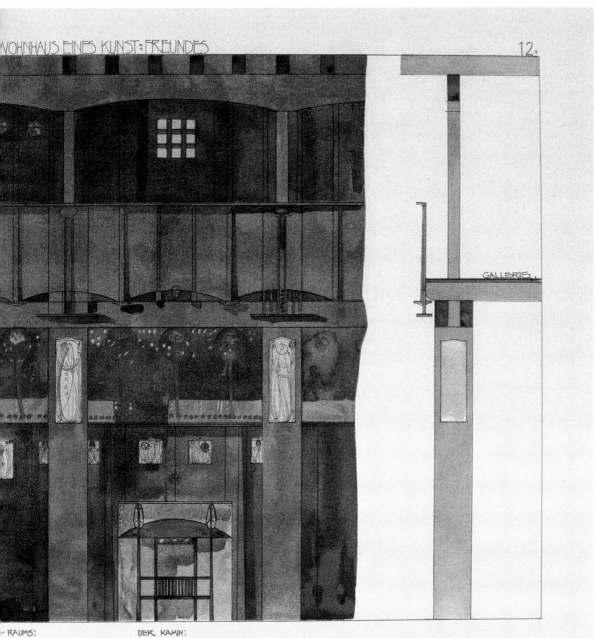

WOHNHAUS EINES KUNST-FREUNDES                                          12.

GALLERIE.

-RAUMS:                    DER KAMIN:

C. R. MACKINTOSH. GLASGOW.  HAUS EINES KUNST-FREUNDES.

VERLAGS-ANSTALT: ALEXANDER KOCH-DARMSTADT. - TAFEL XII.

HAUS EINES KUNSTFREUNDES *1901*

## DESIGN FOR THE DINING ROOM

*Courtesy of the Hunterian Art Gallery,
University of Glasgow*

IN contrast to the main reception room of the house, the dining room was far more austere in design. Dark panelled walls and dark furniture were relieved by the white vaulted ceiling, the fifteen gesso panels and the pale carpet. The table sat a good number, though it is shown only with two new high-backed armchairs at either end, each with a single central back panel tapering from head to foot.

On the south wall is a sturdy piece of fitted furniture which provided both storage space and a sideboard. At the far west end of the room, the fireplace was one of Mackintosh's more simple designs, surrounded by long-stemmed roses.

Never one to heap too much severity on his clients, Mackintosh relieved the sombre, even severe nature of the room, with the inclusion of organic motifs in the carpet, the table and chairs. They can even be found in the wall fittings. As was his way, concerned with creating space where possible, Mackintosh ingeniously built the room with a removable partition that divided it from the hall. Thus by simply removing them the spaces could be used as one when the occasion required.

C. R. MACKINTOSH · GLASGOW. · HAUS EINES KUNST-FREUNDE
VERLAGS-ANSTALT: ALEXANDER KOCH-DARMSTADT. · TAFEL XI

## HAUS EINES KUNSTFREUNDES *1901*

# DESIGN FOR THE RECEPTION AND MUSIC ROOM

*Courtesy of the Hunterian Art Gallery,*
*University of Glasgow*

THE design for the music room was undoubtedly the most elaborate that Mackintosh was to produce and occasioned great interest at the time of the competition. It seems likely to have been the spur for Fritz Wärndorfer to commission Mackintosh to design a music salon for him the following year. The room has window bays all the way down the south side, hung with panels decorated by Margaret.

Light streamed into the room, highlighting the elaborate decorative work at the east and west ends in particular. On the west wall was a white piano, above which was an intricate carving combining two birds, trees and flowers, all of which derived from the organ Mackintosh designed for Craigie Hall in 1897. It was flanked by two large figurative panels designed by Margaret which repeat the shapes in the sculpture. At the opposite end of the room was an ornate fireplace flanked by two cupboards.

The sense of being a room within a room was created by the tapering timber uprights at intervals along the north and south walls. The furniture was minimal but its angular lines contrasted with the many organic shapes and symbols. The whole room was to be painted white, with spots of rose, green, silver, blue and purple creating a harmonious and elegant whole. The influence of Margaret is sensed strongly here, not just because of her panels but because of the overwhelming feminine sensibility of the room.

# HOUSE FOR AN ART LOVER *1989–96*

## FAÇADE

*Courtesy of David Churchill/Arcaid*

FOR 90 years Mackintosh's plans for the Haus Eines Kunstfreundes remained unrealised, then in 1989 Graham Roxburgh, an engineer who had been involved in the re-creation of Miss Cranston's tea rooms, had the idea to build it. It is not known whether Mackintosh had a particular site for the house in mind but serendipity played a hand. A large derelict house, Ibrox Hill House, was languishing in Bellahouston Park, an estate on the fringes of Glasgow. In 1989 it was decided to demolish all but the portico, which was moved to a different position within the park.

The House for an Art Lover was built in the footprint of the original house. It was not a straightforward affair. Mackintosh may have provided the drawings but there were no detailed technical specifications, so a team of architects working under the leadership of Andrew Macmillan embarked on a programme of research to flesh out the gaps, resolving the inconsistencies between the exterior and interior plans. They took their information from clues gleaned from other existing buildings and designs by Mackintosh so they could accurately realise what the judges of the 1902 competition had called the 'impressive cohesiveness between the interior and exterior design'. The house was eventually completed in 1996, an essay in modern geometric style. Owned by Glasgow City Council, it is open to the public and used as a conference centre.

HOUSE FOR AN ART LOVER *1989–96*

## OVAL ROOM

*Courtesy of Eric Thorburn / Glasgow Picture Library*

AT the beginning of the century, it was customary for ladies and gentlemen to withdraw to separate rooms after dinner so the men could smoke and talk before rejoining the women. Mackintosh planned a rectangular gentlemen's room at the south-facing side of the east end of the house. Between it and the music/reception room was the ladies' sitting room – a soft, feminine oval in shape. However, Mackintosh didn't submit any drawings of the room, so it was up to the team working on the realization of the Haus eines Kunstfreundes to interpret what he had provided in the context of the late twentieth century. Their designs were based on the other oval room he had created within the drawing room of Miss Cranston's Hous'hill.

Piers Kettlewell led the team of specialist carpenters and cabinet-makers in their research, which led them to examine the proportions and detailing of Mackintosh's other projects. Everything conforms to the oval shape, from the window to the curves of the wall cabinet, from the overhead light to the radiator. The detail is minutely observed, right down to the tiny square panes of glass in the cabinet doors – 54 in each, all beaded in by hand. Elsewhere in the house the detailing was similarly reproduced, from Margaret's gesso panels and embroideries to the wrought-iron finial on the roof. The house now stands as a testament to Mackintosh's ideal: 'Reason informed by emotion, experienced in beauty, elevated by earnestness, lightened by humour. That is the ideal that should guide all artists.'

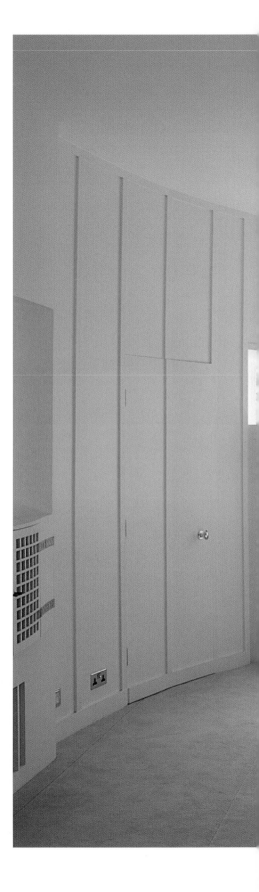

# THE HILL HOUSE, HELENSBURGH *1902–4*

## EXTERIOR FROM THE SOUTH

*Courtesy of the Glasgow Picture Library*

IN 1902 the Glasgow publisher Walter Blackie was searching for an architect to design a house for him and his family on the site he had acquired in prestigious Upper Helensburgh, a short distance from Glasgow. The art director of his publishing company, Talwin Morris, was able to recommend his friend, Charles Rennie Mackintosh. So it was that Mackintosh got the job which must be regarded as the pinnacle of his domestic work.

Mackintosh met with Blackie, who was quite clear about what he wanted: there were to be no red roof tiles and no construction of brick, plaster and wooden beams; the architectural effects were to be achieved by massing the elements, not by the ornamental flourishes the Victorians were so fond of; and there was to be a harling (roughcast) finish. The first designs he saw were for the inside only. Here Mackintosh had taken the lifestyle of the family into account, creating a traditional L-shaped corridor house with the service wing attached to the east end of the long arm of the L. From the outside, the house has a monumental presence, its shapes emphasised but brought together by the unifying silver-grey harling finish under the blue-grey slate of the roof. From the east, the servants' quarters are quite visible, with the children's rooms above and the servants' rooms in the attic.

### THE HILL HOUSE *1902–4*

## ELEVATION FROM THE SOUTH-WEST

*Courtesy of the Glasgow Picture Library*

THE belief that form followed function was central to Mackintosh's philosophy of architecture: that is, his prime concern was that the building must work for the occupants. He designed the interior first in consultation with the Blackie family, making sure that the layout was practical, then he designed the elevations of the building. The windows seem to be randomly placed, but in fact they reflect the importance of the internal composition of the house and form part of an abstract design which balances solid and void. The shell of the house is pierced by 50 windows, 40 of which are completely different, each answering the requirements of the room within and providing variety and play on the exterior walls. Mackintosh was fascinated by using different shapes, but more than that he varied the sizes of the panes from window to window. The Hill House was positioned on a sloping site and he was anxious to integrate it within its surroundings. The south side of the house has the family rooms overlooking the garden. The formality of the west front disappears and the house seems more approachable, with its overhanging eaves and extended gable encompassing the dining room and guest bedroom. Mackintosh jokingly gives heavy stone stutters to the window of the master bedroom, while below the gentle curve of the wall the library window has a particularly deep reveal in contrast. More games are played with the design of the gable end. Beside the symmetry of the main section, it looks impressively abstract, though directions taken by the gable, dormer window and chimney were carefully planned to contradict each other. And there behind it is a traditional Scottish stair tower complete with conical roof.

## THE HILL HOUSE *1902–4*

## MAIN ENTRANCE

*Courtesy of Eric Thorburn*

THE exterior of Hill House shows Mackintosh revelling in the Free Style, bringing different components together to be united in a coherent and modern whole. The principal entrance to the Hill House, on the north-west side, is a fine and perfect example of this, being in direct contrast to so much else that surrounds it.

For such an imposing building, the style of the doorway is strangely modest and retiring. The harling finish comes up to the edge of almost all the openings of the house but not here or on the two windows to one side. William Blackie had been most specific in his brief and insisted upon no ornamentation. Can he have expected such a brutal and unwelcoming treatment of the entrance to the house? Admittedly, once inside the imposing door one is struck with wonder at the design, but this, in contrast to the rest of the interior, is certainly not ornate.

The monumental architrave does convey the solidity and thickness of the walls, presenting Blackie's house as nothing less than his castle (an effect heightened by the portcullis-like effect of the latticework window of the door). By setting the door so far back, Mackintosh underlines the separation between the outside and inside worlds. First, visitors must broach the doorway, before being admitted into the porch within, then moving through heavy lattice doors towards the welcoming hall.

Despite the fashion of the time which would have demanded some ornamental carving, Mackintosh refrained as requested, letting the monumentality of the frame speak for itself, in much the same way as the massing of the different elements of the house does.

### THE HILL HOUSE *1902–4*

# HALL

*Courtesy of Mark Fiennes / Arcaid*

THE hall of the Hill House provides the transition between the rough masculine exterior of the house and its softer, more feminine heart, comprising the white drawing room downstairs and the bedrooms upstairs. The front door at the west end of the building gives into a vestibule and a thick latticework oak doorway which opens into the corridor leading to the hall. The immediate impression is similar to the one received in the Glasgow School of Art as Mackintosh played with strong vertical and horizontal lines, defining the shape of the room and drawing visitors in. It passes the library on the right, where Walter Blackie received callers and had his study. On the left of the hall are the strong vertical solids and voids of the stairway, which leads up to the more private parts of the house, past a partly hidden seat under the upper stair.

The hall itself balances the masculine and feminine elements in Mackintosh's design: light contrasts with dark, tradition with modernity, organic with geometric. Light glints off pink glass inserts in sober dark-stained pine uprights, which are separated by a delicate frieze of tangled organic and geometric motifs faintly reminiscent of those in the Willow Tea Rooms. Here, however, a sinuous shoot breaks out of the confines of the pattern's square. The rectangular brass-framed light fittings include pink and white glass. The white squares are subdivided into rectangles which are topped with a pink rosebud. Through them, the light casts mysterious shadows on the walls above the dark frieze rail, while simultaneously lighting the space below. Though solid, the doors to the rooms beyond are relieved by rectangular glass inserts which hint at something fantastical inside.

THE HILL HOUSE *1902–4*

# HALL: DETAIL OF CLOCK AND CHAIR

*Courtesy of Eric Thorburn / Glasgow Picture Library*

JUST as at Windyhill, the hall of the Hill House was furnished as a reception room. Only family and friends passed through into the heart of the house; everyone else could be seen here or in Mr Blackie's library.

It had never been easy for anyone in Scotland to be a forward-thinker, a moderniser who wished to ignore the traditions and rituals of the country. While Mackintosh strived to create a modern entity out of a traditional form (the family house, in this case), he had to pay attention to the constraints of tradition. Hill House is notable for many things, among them the fantastic timepieces designed by Mackintosh. A cased cabinet clock would have sat in baronial halls and middle-class hallways since they were invented. So at the far end of the hall from the door is a magnificent dark-stained pine clock. It fits elegantly into the geometric patterning that Mackintosh has firmly established in this part of the house. The roman numerals painted on the metal face (very traditional) are fixed by tiny squares which also mark the minutes (very modern). The brass hands and weights (again, traditional) complement the other fixtures and fittings (modern, naturally).

Beside it, the traditionally placed and equally traditionally sturdy unstained oak chair is one of four made for the hall. Its angled latticed back repeats the cutouts on the angular legs of the oval hall table. The thematic presence of the square (that most modern, mathematical shape) is everywhere, from the specially designed carpet to the tiny panes of glass in the door that leads to the servants' quarters and kitchen.

Even the stencilling has succumbed to its influence, the shapes becoming more geometric than organic and including tiny chequered blocks which, once more, echo the traditional tiling effect of hallways and entrance halls the length and breadth of Scotland (and England, too).

### THE HILL HOUSE *1902–4*

# MAIN STAIRCASE

*Courtesy of the Glasgow Picture Library*

ENTERING the Hill House is a transitional experience, moving from the darkness of the porch to the lightness of the hall. Dividing the stairs from the hall are dark timber uprights which recall those of the main staircase in the Glasgow School of Art. Mackintosh played the same games with light and dark, solid and void. Up four steps into the main hall and then turn back to climb another four steps to the main staircase. There he has created a secret sitting area from where a watcher could secretly observe those coming into the house.

The main staircase is in a semicircular curve which, from outside, sets it apart from the rest of the house. It is lit by tall small-paned windows with three stained blue panes at the top of each, with six little pink squares below, underlining another of the contrasts Mackintosh employed so successfully in the house, the rigidity of the geometric against the fluidity of more organic shapes. Coming downstairs, the perspective changes and the emphasis is on the magnificent light fitting below, before being transferred to the horizontal crossbeam and then down into the reception room of the hall.

## THE HILL HOUSE *1902–4*

## STAIR LIGHT

*Courtesy of the Glasgow Picture Library*

MACKINTOSH was as intimately concerned with every detail that contributed to the building of Hill House as he was in all the projects he worked on, as a whole both internally and externally, designing internal features as carefully as he worked on the external structure. Given Mackintosh's concern over use of light, it's natural that the light fittings were a vital consideration in any room he designed, having the power to highlight or detract from a particular area, to create an atmosphere or destroy it if wrongly placed.

His designs varied from the extraordinarily elaborate light fittings in the library of the Glasgow School of Art which were deliberately placed in order to cast maximum light onto the periodicals table, to the simpler solution in 120 Mains Street, where purple glass glints in the gaslight. In every interior he designed, his light fittings are as fascinating and varied as their surroundings. Distinctly and definitely modern, this stair light is a wonderful example of the geometrical patterns he employed so frequently in his designs for the Hill House. The straight edges and mathematical implication of its construction are almost Mackintosh signatures. It is made from nine elongated cubes, each side of which is decorated with nine purplish glass squares. Light bulbs in each of the four corner cubes throw a shadowy light out to the sides, while simultaneously focusing on the stairway below.

In more traditional baronial halls of a previous era in place of these lamps would have been possibly chandeliers or large, ornate iron and glass creations of curves and swirls. As much for decoration as practicality, stair lights of large houses built to make a statement tended to occupy as much of the lofty heights above sweeping stairwells as possible, as if the owner of such a grand house could impose on even the heavens if he so wished. Mackintosh's stair lights for Hill House are more restrained, minimal and essentially modest in comparison.

## THE HILL HOUSE *1902–4*

# DRAWING ROOM: FIREPLACE

*Courtesy of the Glasgow Picture Library*

MOVING from the darkness of the vestibule into the lighter tones of the hall does little to prepare visitors for the exhilarating change of mood on entering the drawing room. Here Mackintosh showed his skill at articulating and interrelating different spaces, so that the character of the room changes with the seasons. Straight in front of the door is the window bay and a summer room, with the music bay to the left. To the right is the largest area, focusing on the fireplace. The carpet adds definition to the three separate 'rooms', its squared design continuing the theme from the hall and establishing areas within the main body of the room.

Mackintosh's fireplaces were always a feat of imagination, quite different from the conventional, often ornamented, marble surround or cast ironwork with tiles. Here the fireplace is gently concave with a glittering mosaic finish and oval mirror inserts. Above it hung a gesso panel by Margaret. The family would gather round this on cold winter evenings with a huge enclosed sofa and chair blocking out draughts and making the area more cosy. On the opposite wall, Mackintosh designed a small window which lit the area without detracting from the real focal point.

### THE HILL HOUSE *1902–4*

## DRAWING ROOM: WINDOW BAY

*Courtesy of the Glasgow Picture Library*

WHEN the summer comes, the drawing room is transformed. Sun pours in through the south-facing windows and the focus of the room is transferred from the fireplace to the window-seat. Extended beyond the formal confines of the room towards the garden, it almost creates a separate room within the whole, the divide made more obvious, as is the case with the music bay, by the way the carpet skims its edge and the fact that the ceiling is lower than in the main room. Built into the recess, the long window-seat flanked by book and magazine racks commands a magnificent view across Helensburgh. Mindful of every detail, Mackintosh built in central heating under the seat just in case. The sides of the seat are marked by timber uprights which rise to the ceiling, combining geometric and organic designs, with square holes punched out under the flower motif at the top. To either side of the seat are tall windows, one of which opens on to the balcony. High on the white panelling are leaded pink and green glass squares echoing the delicate pink motif in the fine curtains.

The dark furniture at first seems incongruous in the room, but the dark wood and light upholstery of the armchairs link the dark and light elements of the room. When the room was completed the dark furniture was confined to the main area, but in 1908 Mackintosh designed the intricate cube table to go here, possibly to tie the separate parts of the room together. Apart from demonstrating his fascination with the square and its possibilities, it also underlines the coexistence of the masculine, geometric side of the house with the lighter, feminine side.

### THE HILL HOUSE *1902–4*

# DRAWING ROOM: MUSIC BAY

*Courtesy of Mark Fiennes/Arcaid*

WITHIN the conventional confines of a large drawing room, Mackintosh created individual spaces for different activities. The music room, with its wooden floor, is a clearly defined space. The frieze rail dictates the height of the lowered ceiling here and in the window bay at right angles to it. It even has its own small window and window-seat.

The fine muslin curtains are delicately patterned to repeat the square motif that appears throughout the house. Discreet is not a word often associated with a grand piano, but its presence in this room is diminished by giving it this space of its own and by introducing similarly toned wooden furniture which contrasts heavily with the lightness of the walls, carpet and upholstery.

Mackintosh's characteristic use of the frieze rail successfully brings all the different areas of the room together. Naturally the space could be turned to use for playing other musical instruments and even as a stage for family entertainments.

THE HILL HOUSE *1902–4*

## DRAWING ROOM: DETAIL OF STENCILLING AND LAMP

*Courtesy of Mark Fiennes / Arcaid*

THIS is one of Mackintosh's characteristically light-filled, white rooms. South-facing, the views were spectacular and light flooded into the room, filtered by the muslin curtains. The walls and ceiling were originally painted white, but when Mrs Blackie decided she wanted the central ceiling lights replaced by wall sconces Mackintosh decided the ceiling would be better painted a deep plummy red to reduce its impact.

The walls are stencilled in pink, green and silvery grey, combining organic and geometric motifs in a stylised rose and trellis pattern. However, the rose head is so stylised it becomes almost abstract. Like the stencilling in the hall, the flowers have become secondary to the grid in which they're placed. The new wall sconces are composed of balanced metal rectangles, the lower half containing a leaded and stained-glass representation of the rose and trellis on the wall.

The standard lamp was added to the room in 1905 and is remarkably modern, futuristic, almost. Its base looks perhaps two decades ahead of its time, with its formal geometric design so familiar to lovers of Art Deco. The squared pattern at the top is made by cunningly juggling the grain of the different pieces of sycamore wood. As if to highlight the perversion of nature in making the top, in strict contrast the shade is embroidered with organic motifs that complement the wall stencil, but none the less still seem to sit rather uncomfortably on the base.

This lamp is a radical and almost shocking attempt by Mackintosh to marry convention with modernism. The fact that the organic motif is unsettled by the stark, angled struts and squared top is proof of how far design had to go before such contradictory forces could be accepted.

### THE HILL HOUSE *1902–4*

## DRAWING ROOM: WRITING CABINET

*Courtesy of the Hunterian Art Gallery,*
*University of Glasgow*

AMONG the furniture that Mackintosh designed for the drawing room were two cabinets that stand out as being among his finest pieces of furniture. The writing cabinet was made for Walter Blackie after much discussion and the rejection of two earlier designs. This must surely be one of the most opulent and ornamental pieces he produced. Made of ebonised mahogany, the doors open to reveal the squared mother-of-pearl inlay and the decorated central panel with a stylised organic design featuring buds, petals, leaves and dewdrops. It has been suggested that the opening of this mysteriously dark object to reveal the treasure inside is symbolic of female sexuality. Certainly it reflects the same impulse that governs the design of his domestic interiors, where visitors move through darkness into the light and feminine interiors at the heart of the home. The mother-of-pearl squares are each composed of tinier squares and are used to give cohesion to the piece through the linking arches over the pigeonholes. The rose petals in the central glass panel are repeated on either side of the lower part of the cabinet. When the doors are open, the desk assumes the kimono shape common to some of Mackintosh's designs. Mackintosh had a similar desk made for himself, though he used pearwood instead of mother-of-pearl, the upper part was slightly taller to accommodate drawings and the central panel showed a rose with falling petals. Made for the grand sum of £20 15s 6d, it was sold in 1994 for £793,500.

## The Hill House *1902–4*

# Drawing room: clock

*Courtesy of Eric Thorburn / Glasgow Picture Library*

DURING his lifetime Mackintosh produced over 400 designs for different pieces of furniture, ranging from chairs to hatstands, beds to domino tables, light fittings to clocks. In every interior he designed, the furniture was key to how he managed internal spaces.

In his work at the Hill House, as previously stated, while he was beginning to move away from his use of organic motifs and experiment much more with geometric ones, Mackintosh continued to mix the traditional with the modern. The Blackies continued to commission him for pieces of furniture after they had moved into the house, and in 1905 Mackintosh completed various extra pieces for the drawing room, including this clock. Its design demonstrates Mackintosh's enjoyment of form and the way he can play visual games, exploiting the areas of solid and void. The square face of the clock is inlaid with ivory at the edges, setting off the traditional face painted with roman numerals.

The face is attached to a very modern cube which houses the clockwork and stands on an equally modern hollow square of sixteen cubed legs. This clock is a fantastic visual conceit allowing different interpretations of its form depending on what angle it is viewed from. Look at it from the front and it seems to stand on only five legs, but from the side those legs resemble a small forest! This design served as a prototype for several clocks that Mackintosh designed later for Mr Bassett-Lowke at 78 Derngate. It has also 'inspired' many and varied clock (and watch) designers since then, and can be found echoed in the appearance of clocks displayed in both public spaces and private homes.

## THE HILL HOUSE *1902–4*

### DINING ROOM

*Courtesy of Mark Fiennes/Arcaid*

EVEN though the building of the Hill House came in under budget, Walter Blackie insisted that he could not possibly afford for Mackintosh to make every piece of freestanding furniture in the house. Although Mackintosh did continue to design furniture for some time after the house was finished, his principal contributions were in the drawing room, hall and master bedroom. Blackie used his own furniture in the dining room, which, with its dark pine panelled walls, seemed to accommodate more traditional pieces. However, the fireplace is spectacular even if not one of Mackintosh's more complex designs.

Flanked on either side by south-facing windows with a view across the garden and down towards the Clyde, it rises imposingly to the height of the frieze rail. Stained pine uprights reach up to two rectangular hanging lamps of steel and stained glass which are duplicated on the opposite wall. Between them a polished-steel fire surround is punctured with squares at its foot and contrasting ovals on its face. Above that a cement panel is inlaid with four-square patterns of blue tile forming a striking rectangular border. The whole thing thumbs its nose at the otherwise traditional treatment of a dining room.

### THE HILL HOUSE *1902–4*

# MASTER BEDROOM

*Courtesy of Mark Fiennes / Arcaid*

AT the head of the stairs, six little squares of glass glint from a dark door in invitation to enter the master bedroom. This is a sanctuary, strategically placed away from the hurly-burly of the rest of the house, where everything dissolves into ivory white, even the back of the door. All the furniture is sleek white, smoothly disguising both the materials and the manner of their construction. As with so many of the interiors he designed, Mackintosh has skilfully arranged the spatial relationships of the room so that the function of each area is clearly defined. The most intimate area is the bed recess, where the ceiling is lowered into a barrel vault. The window bay which opens out this womb-like space echoes its curve in reverse, revealing the reassuring thickness of the walls, where curved shutters, each studded with three pink glass squares, shield the windows.

Originally the high bed-head was hung with embroidered panels of tall dreamy women. The dressing area is directly in front of the bed space under the light, with a cheval mirror placed between the two south-facing windows. Mackintosh planned a glass and timber screen to divide the two areas but it was never made. The third area centres on the fireplace, with an elegantly understated settle beside it. Opposite is the washstand. The geometric scheme is softened by the frieze that travels round the room: delicate mauve roses growing up the walls, topped by a mêlée of flower heads fancifully blowing in the wind.

THE HILL HOUSE *1902–4*

## MASTER BEDROOM: DETAIL OF FIREPLACE

*Courtesy of Mark Fiennes / Arcaid*

ANOTHER of Mackintosh's splendidly original fireplaces provides a focus for one part of the bedroom. Three leaded-glass mosaic panels set into a reflective sheet-steel surround echo the designs used on the rose wall stencil and the more abstract washbasin. Above, the lines of the bookshelf are moderated by the wavy line above the central three niches, which also serves to bring the eye back to the centre of the overall design. The contrast between the glittering metal and the soft white surround lends an added edge of sophistication. Next to the fireplace, a deep wall settle is fitted into the corner to the height of the fireplace – an ideal spot for a morning cup of tea.

Where most of his contemporaries would have favoured a busy chintz or floral print, Mackintosh typically chose something far more discreet. Here a plain fabric with a simple geometric design is all that's necessary. The square table is beautifully proportioned, the lower plane punched with the ubiquitous four-square motif, while the turned and tapering legs create an optical illusion, their dimensions seeming to change in accordance with the way the table is turned.

Mackintosh has articulated an elegant and private corner for relaxation away from the other world of the house.

THE HILL HOUSE *1902–4*

## MASTER BEDROOM: DETAIL OF WARDROBES AND CHAIR

*Courtesy of Eric Thorburn / Glasgow Picture Library*

NEXT to the wall settle stand two white-painted wardrobes, their tops reaching the frieze rail. Their necessarily angular nature is complemented by the mouldings, with the long stems of two flower heads passing through a narrow trellis of pink glass. The slight curve at the foot of the stem is reversed within the flower head above. Most disturbing, though, is the black ladder-back chair between the wardrobes. This is one of two identical chairs designed specifically for the bedroom along with a low stool. Made of ebonised oak, the severity of the design and colour jars with the whiteness of the rest of the room, but at the same time draws attention to it by contrast. The chairs look both uncomfortable and fragile so were probably only ever intended to have clothes thrown on them. The unbending horizontal lines of the chair back, topped with its trellis design, underline the geometric nature of the designs in the rest of the room.

Mackintosh uses the chairs deliberately in order to articulate the changing areas of the room, their contrasting masculine lines at odds with the femininity of the rest of the room, yet their flimsiness at odds with the mass of the wardrobes and the flanking walls beside them. The tension between these masculine/feminine, dark/light, organic/geometric qualities is something that Mackintosh had been developing in his work for some time, but it was never used to such great effect as here.

## THE HILL HOUSE *1902–4*

# MASTER BEDROOM: WASHSTAND

*Courtesy of the Glasgow Picture Library*

MACKINTOSH not only designed each piece of furniture for the bedroom but also planned where it would stand. Out of view from the bed recess is the washstand, close to the fireplace for warmth. A simple shape, with a cupboard and slatted shelf for storage, like the rest of the furniture in the room it is painted a sensuous ivory white. Its top surface is painted silver while the stand glitters with patterned glass. The pair of steel bowls and ewers that were kept on top provided a stark contrast with the softness of their surroundings.

The stern angular design of this piece is feminised by little details such as the tiny downward curve in the bottom shelf beneath the meeting of the doors, the stylised roses on the panels by the handles and, of course, the design on the mirror itself. Here, the rose pattern that surrounds the room is transformed by rendering it in geometrical shapes. For an uninterrupted reflection, however, a cheval mirror is placed between the two large windows that light the room from either side. It is similar to a mirror Mackintosh designed for Windyhill, but the pedestals are wider and accommodate the nine-square grid that is echoed on the bed-head and on the wardrobes.

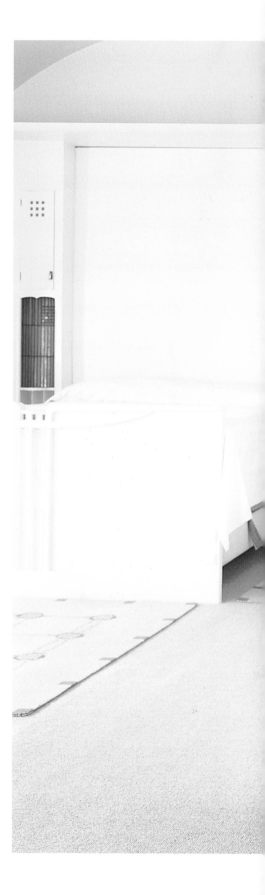

# DRESDENER WERKSTÄTTEN FÜR HANDWERKSKUNST EXHIBITION *1903*

## DESIGN FOR THE BEDROOM FIREPLACE

*Courtesy of the Hunterian Art Gallery,
University of Glasgow*

IN 1903 Mackintosh began to design a bedroom to be exhibited in the Dresdener Werkstätten für Handwerkskunst exhibition. The room was evidently inspired by his ideas for the master bedroom at the Hill House, on which he was working at the same time. However, here the emphasis was entirely on the geometric, the only organic symbolism appearing in embroidered panels over the bed-head. The square was the predominant motif, whether used alone or in groups to form another square, as seen in the chair backs or round the fireplace. The total commitment to these shapes tempered the room's elegance with an air of severity absent from its counterpart. The walls below the frieze rail were pale grey, with darker squares stencilled on them, which immediately dictated a different atmosphere from the dazzling white of the Hill House.

The three high-backed chairs were painted white, making them look even more spindly and frail than their prototypes, while the other furniture was also uncompromisingly geometric in design. It is unclear why Mackintosh adopted such a strong emphasis on the right angle rather than the curve at this point in his career. He may have been responding to the enthusiasms of progressive designers working in Germany and Austria, or perhaps a natural progress in his work was leading him to abandon the fluid organic forms he had used for so long.

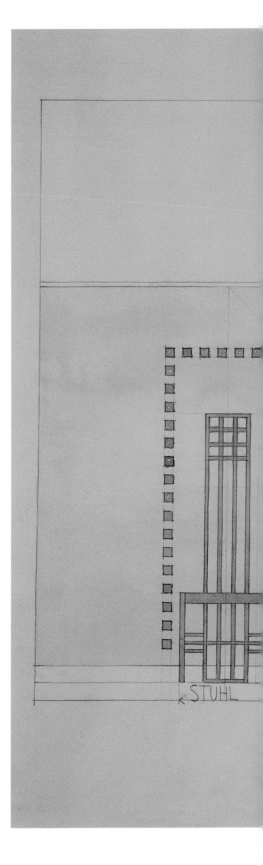

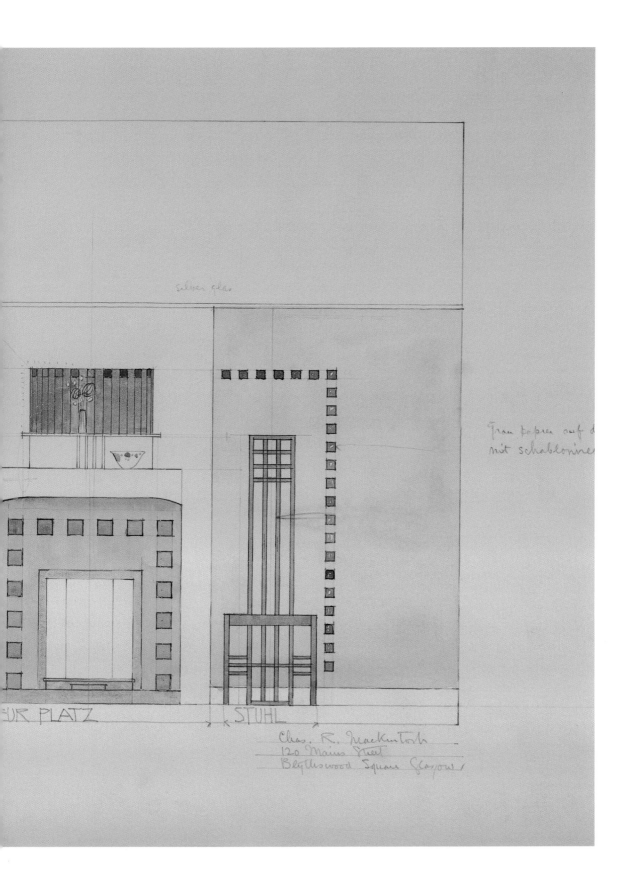

# SCOTLAND STREET SCHOOL, 255 SCOTLAND STREET, GLASGOW *1903–6*

## FRONT ELEVATION

*Courtesy of Eric Thorburn / Glasgow Picture Library*

THE Scotland Street School was Mackintosh's last public commission in Glasgow. The Scottish Education Board was extremely specific in its requirements and, more importantly still, its budget. Mackintosh was to adhere to the standard arrangement in schools of the day, with separate entrances for girls, boys and infants, three floors of classrooms on either side of a corridor running east–west, and a central assembly hall.

He rose to the challenge with typical ingenuity, using the traditional elements but adding his own idiosyncratic twist. Mackintosh planned the hall and classrooms in the central part of the building, using larger windows for the hall and smaller for the classrooms, with a cornice to divide the attic storey in a conventional manner. At either side are two stair towers with conical roofs in Scottish vernacular style, but then he did something different. Instead of tiny windows, Mackintosh reversed tradition and gave them walls of glass with narrow stone mullions. Instead of spiral stairs, he used straight flights, which benefit from the light that streams into them.

Here again, as in so much of his work, Mackintosh played off the verticality of the towers against the horizontal nature of the rest of the building, just as he did with the tower of the Glasgow Herald Building. Beside them, he unusually stepped back the mezzanine floors which contained the cloakrooms and teachers' rooms.

## SCOTLAND STREET SCHOOL *1903–6*

## REAR ELEVATION

*Courtesy of Eric Thorburn / Glasgow Picture Library*

THE rear of the school is, in contrast to the front, almost completely flat, with eighteen uniform windows lighting the classrooms. It is here that the limitations imposed by the brief and budget become all too apparent.

All the variations and play in light and materials one expects from a Mackintosh building are absent, except for the subtle detailing. The classically formal (almost Georgian) rear aspect seems almost more appropriate for the front of a building, while it could be argued that the front looks more like a conventionally designed back of a building.

Proof of the modernist styling and forward-thinking of Mackintosh is provide by the stepped-back mezzanine floors at the front of the building which anticipate architectural developments of the modern movement – at which point they became a common enough feature. The towers presaged the glass and metal stairwells used by Walter Gropius for his Werkbund factory, exhibited in 1914.

Not that Mackintosh's genius was wholly appreciated by his clients at the time. As is the way of bureaucrats throughout the world, the school governors objected strenuously to the cost of cleaning so many panes of glass. They can't have been impressed with the fact that the project came in at 25 per cent over budget, and duly complained about it. Unfortunately, this was only one of a number of complaints that had begun to come in from clients about Mackintosh's overspending. All of which began to make John Keppie reluctant to entrust Mackintosh with jobs on his own.

Continuing to be unappreciated, the school was threatened with demolition in the 1970s but was thankfully transformed into a museum of education which opened in 1990.

## SCOTLAND STREET SCHOOL *1903–6*

# DETAIL OF THE REAR ELEVATION

*Courtesy of Eric Thorburn / Glasgow Picture Library*

AS with all of Mackintosh's designs, the genius is in the detail. A nice touch is the central infants' entrance, which is scaled down in size so as not to be too intimidating. The main doorways are finished with exaggerated architraves to signify their importance. Two sets of four-square green enamel tiles mark the entry. The central bottom pane of each of the penultimate row of windows in the stair towers contains a leaded triangle, and the flanking panes in the row below are leaded with tiny squares. Similarly, a circular leaded-glass motif exists in the bottom smaller-paned windows. The stonework between the top windows is carved, while to the side of them a succession of similar vertical mouldings creates a band marking the top of the tower.

All these features succeed in adding life to the otherwise relatively austere sandstone and glass façade. The railings in front of the school contain abstracted organic shapes that are believed to represent thistle seeds, marking the place where the future of Scotland is going to grow. At the back of the school, Mackintosh took the central bay of two windows' width, extends the windows, and manages to create an exceptionally subtle feature thanks to the decorative carving and tiled symbols which relieve the overwhelming severity of the façade. The Viennese influence can be seen in the abstraction of the tree of life and thistle motifs, which are created out of raised cubes, some with green glazed surfaces, and triangles.

# THE WILLOW TEA ROOMS, 217 SAUCHIEHALL STREET, GLASGOW *1903–4, 1917*

## FAÇADE

*Courtesy of Eric Thorburn / Glasgow Picture Library*

THE site chosen for the last tea room that Mackintosh was to work on with Miss Cranston was in Sauchiehall Street. 'Sauchiehall' means 'alley of the willows' and throughout the rooms he used the willow as a motif. Significantly, this was the only one of his tea rooms where Mackintosh designed the exterior of the building as well as the interior. He removed all the mouldings and added a curved section on the second and third floors, giving the windows unusually deep reveals. He put a landscape window with small square panes in on the ground floor and smaller windows with stained-glass willow leaves above. Small squares decorate the sides of the façade and underneath the ground-floor window. Assuming an implacably modern air, the Willow Tea Rooms immediately looked like nowhere else in Glasgow.

Inside, there was plenty of space to allow a similar arrangement to the Ingram Street or Argyle Street Tea Rooms. On the ground floor, the ladies' tea room was at the front, with a lunch room at the back. The vaulted room on the first floor above the tea room was transformed into Mackintosh's most magnificent tea room of all, the Salon de Luxe, where Margaret's influence is clearly evident. Upstairs was used exclusively by men who patronised the billards and smoking rooms.

In 1917 Mackintosh designed and added the Dug Out, a brightly coloured fantasy in the basement. This photograph shows the building today, now a jewellery shop.

## THE WILLOW TEA ROOMS *1903–4*

# SALON DE LUXE

*Courtesy of the Hunterian Art Gallery,*
*University of Glasgow*

THE vaulted room at the top of the Willow Tea Rooms was known as the Salon de Luxe and was Mackintosh's most lavishly decorated tea room. It is a further example of how the Mackintoshes adapted the ideas they had already used in domestic settings: in this instance, the more sophisticated treatment of their designs for House for an Art Lover or for 14 Kingsborough Gardens.

The walls below the glass frieze were lined with purple silk stitched with beads, while the seats were upholstered in purple velvet. The long window overlooking Sauchiehall Street was decorated with mirrored shapes resembling willow leaves which can be seen from the outside.

On the wall opposite the fireplace was an elaborate gesso panel by Margaret that continues the willow theme: *O Ye, All Ye That Walk in Willow Wood*, from a sonnet by Dante Gabriel Rossetti. This was a room designed specifically for women's enjoyment. When it opened, it was described in a Glasgow weekly as 'simply a marvel of the art of the upholsterer and decorator'.

### THE WILLOW TEA ROOMS *1903–4*

## GLASS FRIEZE

*Courtesy of Eric Thorburn / Glasgow Picture Library*

THE theme of young willow trees was continued throughout the Willow Tea Rooms. Mackintosh used a favourite medium, leaded stained glass, to embellish a mirror frieze that ran around the room above the dado rail. From a distance the untrue lines and leaf-like motifs give the impression of a natural maze, its patterns rectangular but not mathematical.

Stylised willow trees were clearly represented by the purple and white leaded glass. The colours matched those used in the room and reflected the elegance of the furnishings. Yet the design on the mirror is sufficiently subtle to create a sense of space and light, both definite imperatives for Mackintosh. Of course, the mirror also gave those sitting with their back to the centre of the room a good view of what's going on behind them. It helped immensely to allow a sense of movement round the room, from the expanse of window to the elaborate stained–glass door.

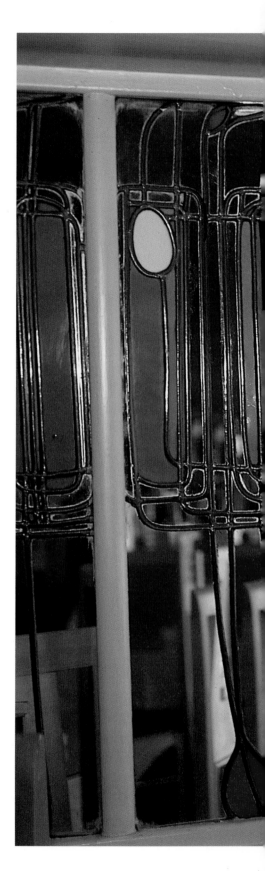

## THE WILLOW TEA ROOMS *1903–4*

# DOORS TO THE SALON DE LUXE

*Courtesy of the Hunterian Art Gallery, University of Glasgow*

THE Salon de Luxe was the culmination of the rooms Mackintosh designed for Miss Cranston. Its entrance was accordingly magnificent and represents his finest and most complex work, combining lead and stained glass. The door led into the room which Mackintosh designed entirely, thus lending to the unity of the whole creation.

Where previous Mackintosh designs combined the formal and masculine exterior with more feminine interiors (see the Hill House, page 136), with the Salon Mackintosh ditches the formal, mathematical approach for a natural, softer overview. The design of the doors stretched sideways from the handles creating a pattern resembling the shape of a kimono, but the delicate design repeated the theme of stylised willows and includes two pink roses. This theme is, of course, continued across the mirrored glass frieze inside the Salon.

Mackintosh borrowed from Celtic art, in which abstracted plant forms are shaped in a similar way. The imagery principally functioned through the use of colour and light. Think of the play of light on the glass as the door swings back and forth with the carefully uniformed waitresses scurrying about their business. The beaten-metal door plates repeated the pattern set up in the glass, while the handles are elegantly twisted to the right and left.

Inside the Salon was perhaps its pièce de résistance: in the middle of the room hung a splendid glass chandelier made up of rose-coloured baubles that dangled loosely around a light. The rose-tinted light cast softly across the room on a wet, cold and dark winter's afternoon must have been magnificently warm and welcoming. Sadly, the chandelier no longer exists.

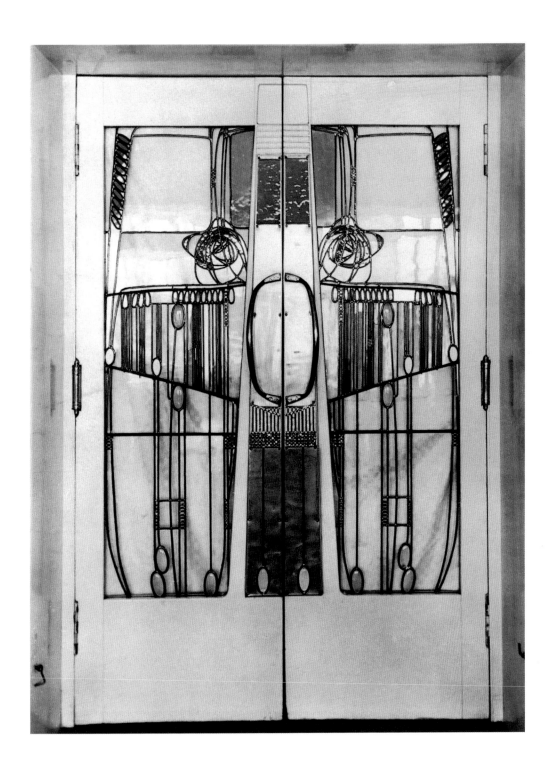

## THE WILLOW TEA ROOMS *1903–4*

# DRAWING FOR CHAIR AND TABLE IN THE SALON DE LUXE

*Courtesy of the Hunterian Art Gallery,
University of Glasgow*

EACH aspect of the Salon de Luxe came under Mackintosh's scrutiny. These designs demonstrate the thought that went into every detail. He used eight high-back chairs, four at each of the two tables in the centre of the room, to create a sense of privacy for the diners who sat there and to subdivide the room further. But gone is the heavy oak of the Argyle Street Tea Rooms.

These chairs were painted silver and upholstered in purple velvet with six squares of pink glass cut high into their backs. The squares were repeated round the edge of the grey carpet in the centre of the room. The only organic motifs to be found were the stylised willow leaves carved into the table legs. Around the edges of the room Mackintosh used silver-painted chairs with lower backs to face the banquettes. These designs contributed to a sybaritic and luxurious atmosphere that pampered the women of Glasgow, who came to talk and eat in sobriety.

When the tea rooms opened their doors for the first time in 1904 the verdict was unanimous and Miss Cranston's choice of architect/designer entirely vindicated. The *Glasgow Evening News* trumpeted, 'Until the opening of Miss Cranston's new establishment in Sauchiehall Street today the acme of originality had not been reached.'

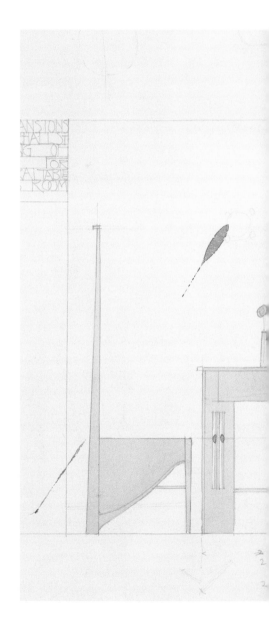

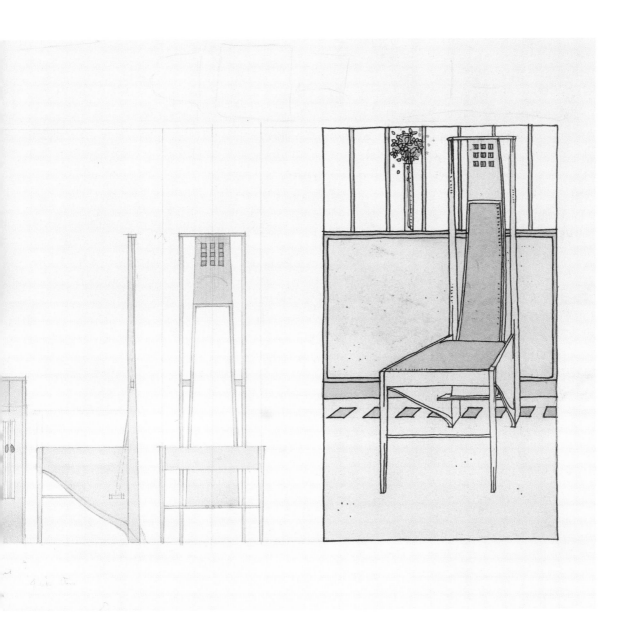

## THE WILLOW TEA ROOMS *1903–4*

# FRONT SALON

*Courtesy of the Glasgow Picture Library*

FOLLOWING their masculine–feminine coding, the Mackintoshes gave the front tea room a colour scheme of white, silver and rose, while the mixed lunch room at the back of the same floor was panelled with dark oak and grey canvas. In the tea room, the wall panelling, screens, fireplace, ceiling and plaster relief frieze were all painted white. In contrast, the dark wood of the high ladder-backed chairs stood out, dividing the room into separate areas. The most extraordinary subdivision of all was in the centre of the room, where a curious timber structure enclosed two tables for two. At the top of the timber uprights were panels carved with stylised willow leaves.

The whole was topped by a large glass bowl for long-stemmed flowers, which was in turn surrounded by a similar but four-legged structure in metal. It has been suggested that this was intended to represent a willow tree, but no record has been found to support the theory. Similarly, the angular patterns repeated on the plaster panels making up the frieze represented a willow tree, though without knowing it this would not be easy to interpret. The unique light fitting consisted of unshaded bulbs attached at intervals to a circular band of flat metal suspended from the ceiling by large hoops.

## THE WILLOW TEA ROOMS *1903–4*

# GALLERY TEA ROOM

*Courtesy of the Hunterian Art Gallery,*
*University of Glasgow*

AT the back of the Willow Tea Rooms was a single-storey extension which Mackintosh used for the general lunch room. Its ceiling was lower than that belonging to the room at the front of the building, so he was able to fit a gallery along the three external walls. The fourth had a decorative glass and metal screen which filled the gap between the two levels. This skilful shaping of the space allowed an awareness of the other dining areas, giving a sense of connection with them while simultaneously remaining separate.

The tea gallery had roses stencilled on the walls below the frieze rail, while the china used here, as elsewhere in the tea rooms, was none other than the appropriate willow pattern. Eight tapering columns rose from the gallery and the supporting beams to the exposed beams of the ceiling above. The posts were square at the base and circular at the top, where they were surrounded by four lampshades. The roof above the four central pillars was solid but light flooded down through the glazed roof at the sides of the gallery and on to the tables below.

THE WILLOW TEA ROOMS *1903–4*

# LATTICE-BACKED CHAIR

*Courtesy of the Glasgow School of Art Collection*

THIS is one of Mackintosh's most original and impressive chairs, designed as a unique piece for the Willow Tea Rooms. His awareness of the spatial possibilities of the premises led Mackintosh to use the furniture to subdivide the area without forming solid barriers to block the sightlines. Almost as if he was placing pieces on a chessboard, Mackintosh created the whole entity as an elaborate, near-mathematical creation with every component playing its part.

The most important person in the tea rooms (the Queen, if you like) was the manageress and this was her chair, located between the front and back salons, where she sat taking orders and conveying them to the kitchen by a system of coloured balls which she dropped down a tube into the basement. Even when she was not sitting down, the chair had the architectural function of marking the divide between the cool whiteness of the front room and the dark furniture of the general dining room at the back.

Made of ebonised oak, the latticework on the back is a symbolic representation of – once again – a willow tree. The severe geometric structure is softened by the way it is curved round the seat to embrace the sitter. In the dining room, the furniture echoed the strong rectilinear feel of this chair. Round the edges under the gallery were tables flanked by dark ladder-backed chairs, while in the centre were tables placed at an angle, each with four low-backed armchairs. A final touch is provided by the carpet, with its chequered design clearly marking out the aisles.

THE WILLOW TEA ROOMS *1917*

# THE DUG OUT

*Courtesy of the Glasgow School of Art Collection*

THE last commission Mackintosh completed in Glasgow was, perhaps appropriately, for his long-time patron Miss Cranston. In 1917 she proposed to extend her Willow Tea Rooms into the basement of the building next door. Mackintosh simply took out the fireplace in the front salon and introduced a staircase to connect the two. Miss Cranston patriotically named the new tea room the Dug Out, in reference to the trenches. The dim light and subterranean atmosphere lent themselves to the wartime theme. Mackintosh had begun to use more exotic designs and bright colours, following the influence of the Viennese Secession, a breakaway group of artists from the Künstlerhaus.

He had used bright primary colours on the chamfered balustrades in the School of Art library, and his creation of the Chinese Room for Miss Cranston had been an exotic combination of form and colour, with its brilliant blue latticework and black chairs. However, the real inspiration for the Dug Out was his design for the hall at 78 Derngate. Once again Mackintosh took a domestic interior and exploited it in a commercial setting. He used the same male coding of the hall and painted the walls and ceiling a dramatic velvety black, but relieved it with areas of brilliant colour – vivid blue stripes in geometric patterns, relieved by touches of red and green, as well as zigzagging yellow triangles outlined with white.

### THE WILLOW TEA ROOMS *1917*

# THE DUG OUT: YELLOW SETTLE

*Courtesy of the Glasgow School of Art Collection*

THE focal point of the room was the stunning memorial fireplace which was decorated with inlaid glass and paintings of flags of the opposing warring nations neatly ranged on either side. Above it was a wall panel painted with triangles, diamonds and checks in vivid red, blue and green. The black-and-white chequered lattice was as conspicuous as it was both in the Dutch Kitchen and at 78 Derngate. Once again, it led up to a bold design of inverted yellow triangles. Placed behind the seat, they could be interpreted as stylised trees.

No photographs have survived of the room, unfortunately, only some of Mackintosh's drawings and a few pieces of furniture. The latticework settle is a version of the one in the Derngate bay window, but instead of black Mackintosh chose to have it painted a vibrant chrome yellow, adding bright purple upholstery. The armchairs were heavy, narrower at the back than at the front, with a modified ladder-back and a bobbin between two cubes carved to support the armrests above the seat. Similarly the tables used bobbins or a combination of cube and bobbin for their legs.

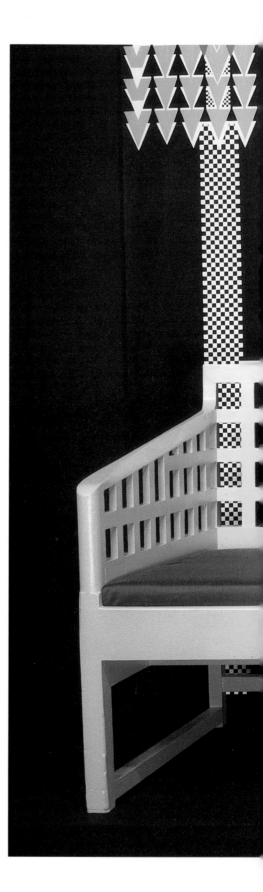

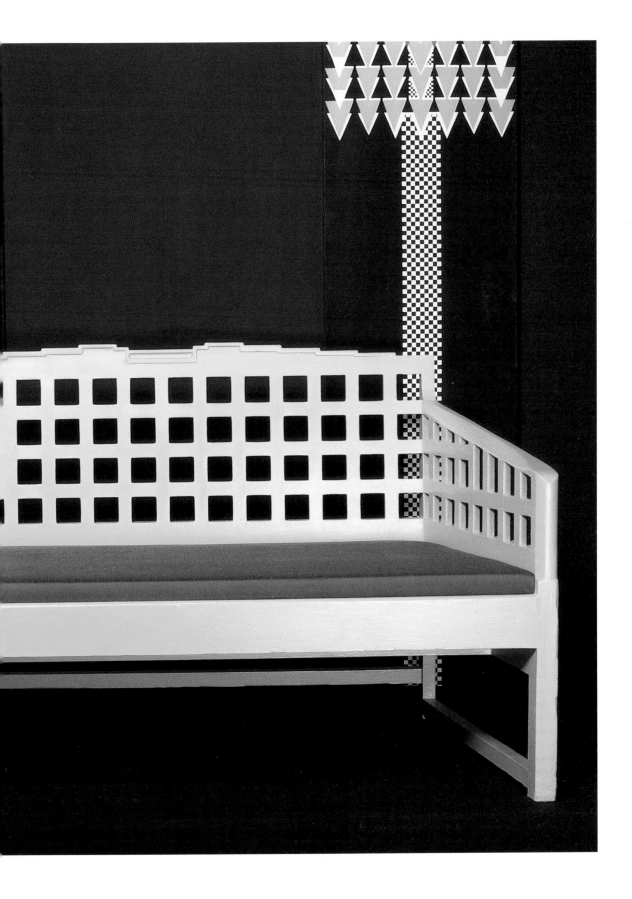

THE WILLOW TEA ROOMS *1914*

# THE DUG OUT: THE LITTLE HILLS BY MARGARET MACDONALD MACKINTOSH, OIL ON CANVAS

*Courtesy of the Hunterian Art Gallery, University of Glasgow*

ANOTHER way of alleviating the basement gloom of the Dug Out was to use two large oil paintings by Margaret. She had begun them with the help of her husband while they were living in Walberswick. This one was based on the 65th Psalm:

*Thou crownest the year with thy goodness;*
*And thy paths drop fatness.*
*They drop upon the pastures of the wilderness;*
*And the little hills rejoice on every side.*
*The pastures are clothed with flocks;*
*The valleys are covered over with corn;*
*They shout for joy, they also sing.*

It exhibits quite a different feeling from the dreamy, sinister paintings of her youth. The figures are quite clear and rather chubby, the colours vibrant and strong. This is a joyous and optimistic song of praise to nature and its fecundity. Rather than concentrating on the dark fatalism of so much being affected by the Great War, Margaret has hinted at the terrible loss and suffering being endured by 'our boys' across the Channel without actually depicting it. These almost inhuman but somehow jolly figures manage to convey a sense of hope along with a sense of doom, as if they are the souls of the lost ascending to heaven above the fields of death and their journey is a happy one. As the psalm can be interpreted for the time, where the dead fall they shall be the goodness from which joy will grow.

# HOUS'HILL, NITSHILL, GLASGOW *1904*

### DESIGN FOR CHAIRS

*Courtesy of the Hunterian Art Gallery,*
*University of Glasgow*

IN 1903 the tireless Miss Cranston and her husband, Major John Cochrane, decided to do up the interior of their home in the southern outskirts of Glasgow. The obvious man for the job was Mackintosh, since he had made such a success of her tea rooms. He made no alterations to the structure of Hous'hill, but the commission provided him with the opportunity to design a wide range of furniture. In all his designs he showed an even greater awareness of geometric form than before, whether designing for the two upstairs bedrooms or for the drawing room and hall below. He divided the drawing room by introducing a semicircular open screen to separate the sitting room from the music room, once again playing with spatial organization and interrelating spaces.

The chairs were made of beech or sycamore, stained dark, their stylish back-rails in a subtle curve and studded with inserts of coloured glass. Four lower-backed versions were commissioned and an armchair, surely one of the most elegant of Mackintosh's chairs, which was sold in the 1970s at Sotheby's for £9,200.

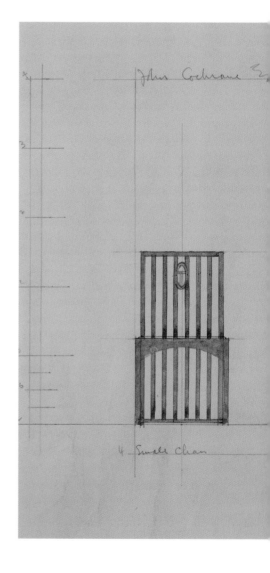

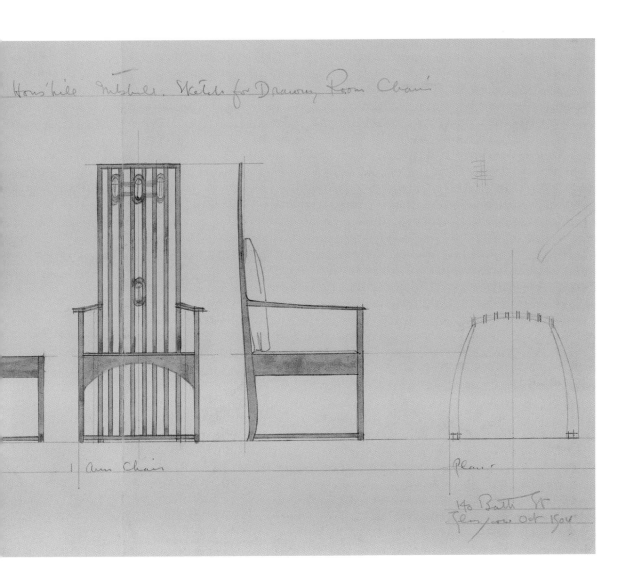

Hous'hill Mitchell. Sketch for Drawing Room Chair

1 Arm Chair

Plan

140 Bath St
Glasgow Oct 1904

## HOUS'HILL, NITSHILL, GLASGOW *1904*

# THE WHITE BEDROOM

*Courtesy of the Hunterian Art Gallery,*
*University of Glasgow*

MACKINTOSH redecorated two bedrooms at Hous'hill. The walls and ceiling of the blue bedroom were painted white and stencilled, but the furniture was dark and geometric, marking a radical departure from his feminine white rooms at Mains Street and the Hill House. The decorative features emerged from linear design, the repeated theme of the square and the exposed grain of the wood. However, in the white bedroom he drew on the designs he made for the bedroom in the Dresdener Werkstätten für Handwerkskunst exhibition, establishing a geometric formality that is common to the two.

The bedroom and furniture were largely painted white, complying with his feminine coding, but the sensual erotic nature of the Hill House bedroom was not repeated. The room worked to a careful grid whereby the light fittings, stencilling and bed-top were at the same height and repeat the same images, an identical stylised motif on each. Lower down, the window sill acted as a leveller for the chests of drawers, tables and chair-tops. The furniture was placed round the edge of the room, with the exception of two ebonised chairs which mark the boundary between the sleeping area and the rest of the room.

Despite their understated design, they did little to anchor the room in the way of the ladder-backed chairs at the Hill House. The sense of formality was overwhelming and marks an important transitional moment in Mackintosh's career. Hous'hill was his last domestic commission in Scotland. Sold after Miss Cranston's death in 1920, the house was later destroyed by fire.

# 78 SOUTHPARK AVENUE, GLASGOW *1906*

## THE HALL

*Courtesy of the Hunterian Art Gallery, University of Glasgow/Michael Kuzmak*

IN 1906 Mackintosh and Margaret moved from their Mains Street flat to a house at 6 Florentine Avenue in the prestigious area of Hillhead, close to the university. (Florentine Avenue was later renamed Ann Street and then Southpark Avenue, the number of the house changing from 6 to 78.) After Mackintosh's death, the house was bought by William Davidson, who gave it to the Hunterian Art Gallery. The original building was demolished but they have recreated the interiors in the Mackintosh House, a block away from the original.

It is not known why Mackintosh and Margaret decided to move; perhaps they just wanted the status and security afforded by a house of their own. The end-of-terrace three-storey house with attic stood on a street corner with a south-facing gable end. Mackintosh made a few structural alterations, one of which was to replace the front door. He removed outer storm doors and the existing internal front door and replaced them with a narrower front door with four square lenses glinting from the streetlight. Internally, the removal of the old doors left the hall too wide for the new one. Mackintosh remedied this by inserting some bowed panelling which narrows the hall towards the front door. No records exist as to the decoration but it is thought that probably the coarse grey or brown paper used on the attic stairs was repeated here.

## 78 SOUTHPARK AVENUE *1906*

# DINING ROOM

*Courtesy of the Hunterian Art Gallery, University of Glasgow/Michael Kuzmak*

THE dining room was off the hall to the right and closely resembled its predecessor in Mains Street. Mackintosh removed the cornice and lined the walls to the frieze rail with brown wrapping paper, abandoning the timber uprights he had used before. However, this time the paper was stencilled with a black trellis and pink roses overlaid with green and silver ovals, a pattern he had first used in the hall of Hous'hill two years earlier. The walls and ceiling above were painted white. Gas was replaced by electricity, so the light fixtures were quite different with three pendant lights hanging down in the centre of the room. The Mackintoshes brought the fireplace with them from Mains Street and used the same dining-room furniture.

Though light filtered in through muslin curtains, the atmosphere was subdued compared with the vitality and light of the drawing room upstairs. As with their decoration of 120 Mains Street, the Mackintoshes ingeniously combined old and new, light and dark, masculine and feminine. They didn't need to rip out the old interiors but succeeded in modifying them to create spaces that imply an almost spiritual journey from darkness to light. It is perhaps slightly surprising that they didn't attempt anything more radical in decorating a second home after the work Mackintosh had carried out in the years between. Perhaps they felt that they had perfected a particular vision with which they were entirely comfortable. Equally it has been suggested that Mackintosh may have been tailoring his creativity to comply with what pleased Margaret.

## 78 SOUTHPARK AVENUE *1906*

# DRAWING ROOM/STUDIO

*Courtesy of the Hunterian Art Gallery, University of Glasgow/Michael Kuzmak*

THERE were two rooms on the first floor which Mackintosh knocked through to make an L-shaped drawing room-cum-studio. The entrance was through the studio door, which was studded with purple glass hearts at the back of the house and opened into the wide drawing room at the front. On the east gable-end wall, Mackintosh introduced a low horizontal square-paned window to the height of the flat frieze rail that ran round the room, with small glass squares shining from it as it passed the window.

He used the same techniques to manipulate the space as he had in Mains Street, lowering the room with the rail and hanging the lights at its level. However, this time he went one step further: when the rail reached the window and the bay, he carried it straight across and boxed in the spaces above. In this way he maintained the façade of the building in keeping with the rest of the street, while matching the window heights within the room and seeming to lower it. The rail continued round the studio area but ran straight across the west-facing window without it being boxed in above. This was partly because of the structural problems involved, but also because all possible light was needed in that part of the room. Mackintosh contented himself with inserting more glass insets into the rail, to be lit from the window behind. They took much of the furniture and fittings from Mains Street with them, including the fireplace (without the same grate).

## 78 SOUTHPARK AVENUE *1906*

# BEDROOM

*Courtesy of the Hunterian Art Gallery, University of*
*Glasgow/Michael Kuzmak*

MACKINTOSH turned the two bedrooms on the second floor of the house into one blunt L-shaped room which is painted white. The fireplace and furniture were all brought from 120 Mains Street. He placed the bed in the back part of the L, the most intimate corner of the room. This left the front part as a dressing room, making more space to accommodate the furniture than before. It is thought that the washstand placed against the windows was cut down so as not to obscure the light, but otherwise the pieces remained the same. The door was pierced with eighteen glass hearts that change colour as the light plays on them – a romantic symbol of their affection.

The Mackintoshes left the house in 1914, selling it to William Davidson five years later. It stood untouched until 1945, when it was sold to the Hunterian Art Gallery. By the end of the 1950s the expansion of the university made the demolition of the house inevitable. However, it was carefully dismantled and recreated in a similar building in Hillhead Street. Wherever possible the original has been used, right down to the panelling, the banisters and window sashes.

To enter it is to step back in time, to experience the breathtakingly novel and aesthetic domestic setting Mackintosh and Margaret created for themselves.

**78 SOUTHPARK AVENUE** *1906*

# CHEVAL MIRROR

*Courtesy of the Hunterian Art Gallery, University of Glasgow/Michael Kuzmak*

THIS cheval mirror was designed specifically for the bedroom at 120 Mains Street. Familiarly for Mackintosh, he created a fabulous piece of work based on the use of light within a large project. This is undoubtedly one of Mackintosh's finest pieces of furniture, combining simplicity and elegance, and versatile enough to be taken out of its intended habitat and work gloriously elsewhere. It is both strong enough and flexible enough in its execution to withstand being placed practically anywhere and with anything. One commentator on the Vienna Secession Exhibition apparently compared it to a giant sledge standing on its end, while the design historian David Brett saw its sensuous curve as the forward thrust of a female hip, thus in a swipe making it Margaret's mirror.

However it was intended, the gentle slope of the sides from the wide base to the narrow top has a satisfyingly sculptural appeal. By the top of the mirror and above are two delicate carvings – a moulded stem culminating in a flower bud. They are presumably part of the imagery that was so personal to the Four whose meaning remains uncertain to those outside the group.

None the less, the sense of nature and growth lends another dimension to this stylish piece of furniture. The small drawers contained within the sloping sides hint at other, smaller secrets. What could possibly exist that fits into the pockets of a mirror? More to the point, what could one want to exist to be put in such drawers? It could be something as dull as thread or ribbon or even make-up, or it could be something more precious and mysterious. Along with the carvings these drawers offer strange talking points on what is essentially a vanity mirror.

# 78 DERNGATE, NORTHAMPTON *1916–19*

## STENCIL FOR THE HALL

*Courtesy of the Hunterian Art Gallery,
University of Glasgow*

W. J. Bassett-Lowke was a manufacturer of scale-model machines and railway engines who was making a lot of money producing precision instruments during the war. He had bought a small Georgian terraced house in Northampton and wanted an architect to renovate it for him. A friend recommended Mackintosh.

The commission for 78 Derngate was the first domestic commission Mackintosh had taken since Southpark Avenue. His job was to put in a bathroom, make the most of the limited space, and refurnish and decorate. On the front of the house he added a bay window and remodelled the front door in a way that is reminiscent of the ziggurat finish on the west door of the Glasgow School of Art, adding stained-glass windows containing the triangles that would characterise the hall. At the back of the house he added a three-floor extension which differed radically from its neighbours. Its combination of geometric shapes and a white finish makes it an extraordinary early precursor of the British modern movement.

The staircase of the house was immediately to the left of the front door. Mackintosh removed it and changed its orientation so that it ran across the middle of the house. This had the effect of making the parlour shallower but wider; it was renamed the hall.

## 78 DERNGATE *1916–19*

# DESIGN FOR THE HALL STENCIL

*Courtesy of the Hunterian Art Gallery,*
*University of Glasgow*

FROM 1903 Mackintosh's designs had begun to feature geometric shapes more strongly than the organic forms of his earlier work. Bassett-Lowke was a great fan of German and Austrian design and Mackintosh was already well aware of the work of the Viennese Secession artists, who were popularizing the use of the geometric form. Up until then, the colours used in his work had been largely soft greys, pinks, greens, purples and blues. The exceptions were the brightly coloured chamfered balustrades in the Glasgow School of Art library and the most recent design he had completed for Miss Cranston in the Ingram Street Tea Rooms, where the exotic Chinese Room contained a vibrant blue latticework structure and a pay desk with black lacquered chairs.

When it came to the hall at Derngate, Mackintosh responded to the challenge by subverting the notion of a conventionally dark hall. He included brilliant colours in the stencilled frieze that sang out from the velvety black walls, ceiling and furniture. Small triangular motifs were coloured golden yellow, edged in grey and contained accents of vermilion, blue, emerald and purple. The frieze was broken at intervals by black-and-white-chequered columns reaching down towards the black-and-white-chequered carpet. In 1920 Bassett-Lowke asked Mackintosh to redecorate in a less intense way. It is thought that the original design was lost on him because he was colour-blind but that his wife and friends persuaded him it was too oppressive.

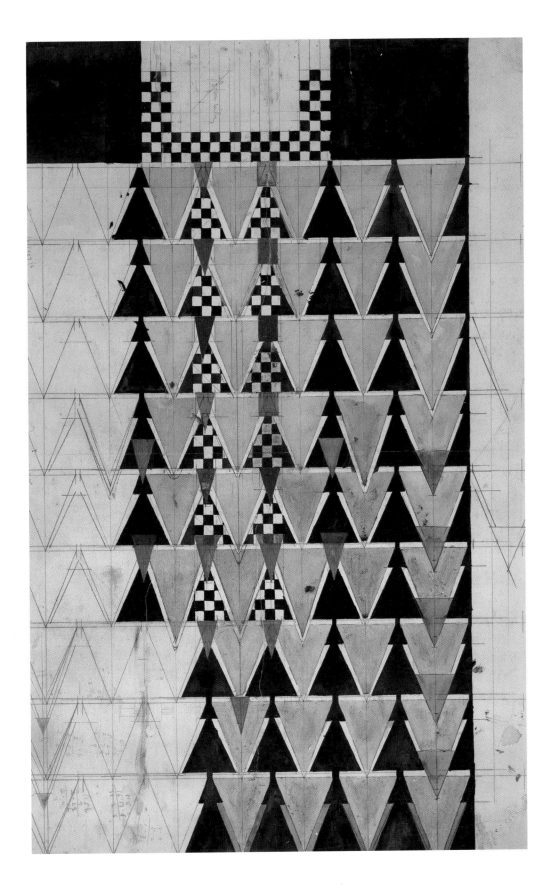

## 78 DERNGATE *1916–19*

## DESIGN FOR STAIR SCREEN AND CUPBOARD

*Courtesy of the Glasgow Picture Library*

THE new stairway ran across the back of the hall and to hide it Mackintosh designed a superb latticework screen employing a combination of square and triangular motifs. The screen was made of timber and used open and closed latticework squares. The open squares at the top of the screen followed the movement of the stairway – yet another example of how Mackintosh could manipulate space, creating boundaries yet maintaining a spatial awareness of what lay beyond. Most of the filled squares were painted the same soft black as the walls and ceiling, but some were filled with chevrons, squares and triangles in coloured glass.

There is no doubt that Mackintosh was influenced in his new designs by what was fashionable in avant-garde German and Austrian design. However, what is less clear is whether Mackintosh wanted to take it to such extremes himself or was encouraged by Bassett-Lowke, who was a huge fan of the work of the Vienna Secession. On the left and right are a standard lamp and chair. The walnut lampstand was the only wood left unpainted in the hall; the triangles on the shade repeat the pattern on the walls. The laquered black chair is characteristic of the rest of the furniture, with its lattice back and decorative detail owing much to Mackintosh's work in Miss Cranston's Chinese Room.

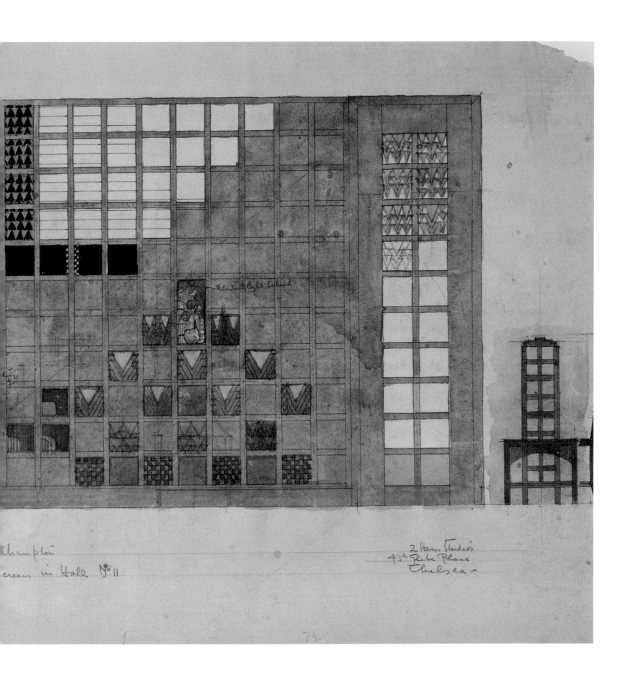

## 78 DERNGATE *1916–19*

# FIREPLACE

*Courtesy of the Hunterian Art Gallery, University of Glasgow*

THE creation of the window bay made extra seating room in the parlour and Mackintosh designed a settle to fit. Distinctly and definitely masculine, it was laquered black with trellis and decorative detailing, and matched the rest of the furniture in the hall, though its vivid pink cushions added life to the room.

The enlarged window flooded the room with light, especially on to the splendid fireplace, which was the room's focal point. The grate resembled several of those in Mackintosh's previous fireplaces but it is the woodwork that is so special. The stepped architrave repeats that used above the front door, with its definite echoes of the west door of the Glasgow School of Art. The edges are familiarly Mackintosh in their mathematical exactness, angularity and darkness.

Above it, the gently convex bookshelf with its wavy top and curved cutouts provides a contradictory sense of fluidity and the usual feminine flourishes. These were the only curves to be seen in the room, apart from the circular central light fitting and the lamp base; everywhere was a mass of geometrical form.

On top sat a bust of George Bernard Shaw, of whom Bassett-Lowke was a particular admirer. What Shaw would have made of Mackintosh's flourishes and the influence of his wife on his work can only be guessed at. One suspects that he would not have approved.

## 78 DERNGATE *1916–19*

## GUEST BEDROOM

*Courtesy of the Hunterian Art Gallery, University of Glasgow*

BASSETT-LOWKE was delighted with the work Mackintosh had done in remodelling his small Northampton terraced house. In 1919 he asked him to return to design the interior of his guest bedroom. The result was one of Mackintosh's most extreme treatments, which relied entirely on geometry and colour to create an effect that belies its theoretical starkness and is never less than welcoming to the visitor.

A black-and-white-striped paper was run up the wall behind the twin beds and on to the ceiling in a dazzling optical illusion, creating the impression of a canopy bed when there is nothing other than paper on the ceiling and wall. Bands of ultramarine harness braid were tacked at regular intervals with black-headed pins on to the edge of the paper and within certain of the stripes. The bed covers repeated the pattern, picking up the use of the ultramarine and adding another accent of bright emerald green. Yet again, it was Mackintosh's use of geometric shapes which defined the space, from the wall and ceiling stripes to the squares that were repeated in the latticework on the side of the stool, the door handles of the cupboard and the pattern decorating the chairs.

Celebratedly severe in its approach, the devotion to the themes of this guest bedroom would appear to indicate the designer was starting to explore new ideas and signatures. Indeed the only curves to be found were in the two bell-like shades which hang over each bed and the natural lines of the pillows under the bed-linen, softer contours that somehow serve to accent the hard lines all around them. Worried that such devotion to style might be too much for at least one of his guests, when showing George Bernard Shaw into the room, Bassett-Lowke is believed to have said, 'I trust the decor will not disturb your sleep,' to which Shaw replied, 'No. I always sleep with my eyes closed.'

225

## 78 DERNGATE *1916–19*

## DESIGN FOR DRESSING TABLE

*Courtesy of the Hunterian Art Gallery,*
*University of Glasgow*

MACKINTOSH used light oak for the furniture in the room, working with the calming natural grain of the wood to make a contrast with the bright angular scheme of the rest of the room. The danger was that the pieces might be overwhelmed by the electrifying decoration, so the designs were all kept simple, using largely undecorated planes of timber. What ornamentation there was was kept to a minimum. Square cutouts and black rectangles were picked out on the bed-feet. The chairs, carefully positioned at the foot of each bed, echoed the blue of the scheme, both in the upholstery and in the plastic inlay.

The emphasis was on the geometric shapes of the pieces, enhanced by black outlining or by the chequered bands on the chairs and stools which added to the vertical emphasis of the room. Even the handles were tiny ebonised squares, frequently inset with mother-of-pearl. The inclusion of the stripes and motifs on the furniture reflects the influence of the Viennese Secession and designers such as Otto Prutscher, Otto Wagner and Josef Urban, whose work Mackintosh must have seen either in his visits to Vienna or in contemporary design periodicals. The pieces were made by German prisoners-of-war in the Isle of Man.

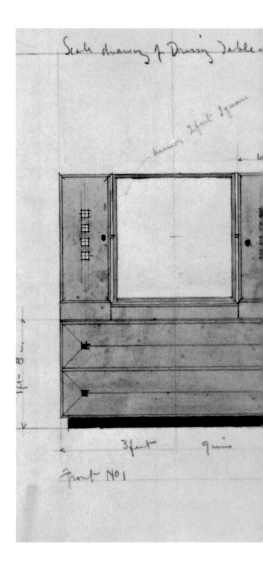

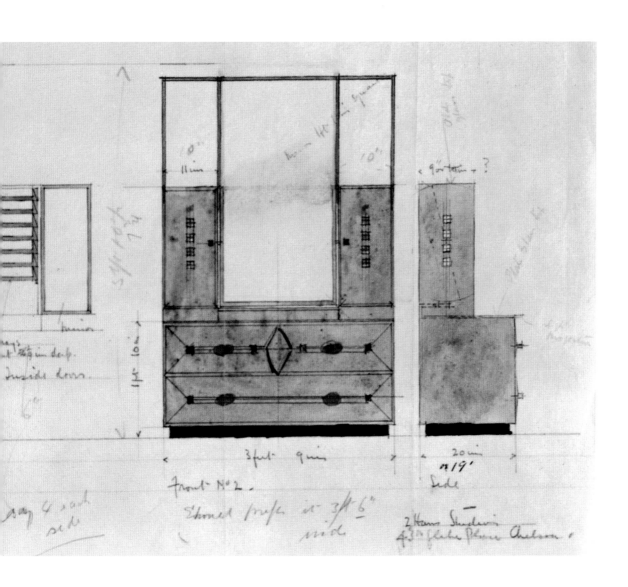

## ORVIETO CATHEDRAL *1891*

*Courtesy of the Hunterian Art Gallery, University of Glasgow*

IN 1890, the year after he completed his articles and was taken on by the Glasgow architectural firm of Honeyman and Keppie, Mackintosh entered a competition for funding for foreign travel in memory of a local architect, The Alexander Thomson Travelling Scholarship. Although the prize of £60 perhaps doesn't seem like much today, over a hundred years ago it was enough to fund several months abroad touring Europe's great cities.

Mackintosh's entry was a design for a public hall executed in perfect classical style in the contemporary building tradition of Glasgow, and he duly won. Never having been outside Great Britain, he decided to go to Italy the following year. He arrived in Naples in April, going on to Sicily, Rome, Umbria and Tuscany, filling sketchbooks and diaries as he went. To begin with he seems to have been more interested in jotting down pencil sketches as aide-memoires, concentrating on architectural details, but as time went by he began to use watercolours more – in his sketches of the cloisters at Monreale, in his scenes of Palermo and in the Arch of Titus in Rome, among others.

He arrived in Orvieto in May and spent five days there. He has clearly been captivated by the different colours of the stone. This is principally an architectural drawing which simply records the patterns found on the surface of the building. It shows little use of imagination, though it does reveal Mackintosh's fascination with the play of light on surfaces.

Ultimately his trip to Italy did little to influence his own work, principally because so much of his work was forward-looking and determined to move into the modern by taking traditions and advancing them. Italy is full of past wonders which have been taken to their conclusion in the execution. Clearly the white stone of Tuscan duomos would have been something of a confirmation and appeared oddly familiar to Mackintosh. He had used the idea of light reflecting from buildings since the *Daily Record* contract. Seeing it as used centuries before by Tuscan architects and builders must have been a pleasant affirmation for him.

ORVIETO.

CRM
1891.

# HARVEST MOON *1892*

*Courtesy of the Glasgow School of Art Collection*

HARVEST *Moon* represents a radical departure from the architectural drawings that Mackintosh had tended to produce until this point. It is the first in a series of works that clearly stem from his imagination. In it he enters a mystical world which has aspects in common with the work of his wife Margaret and Frances Macdonald (even perhaps of William Blake). An angel stands silhouetted against the moon, her wings forming an almost perfect circle around it. Her hair and clothing float round her, blending into the ribbon of cloud that crosses the moon. She is seen through thorny undergrowth peppered with coloured 'berries' which are similar to the leaves depicted in the Salon de Luxe willow glass frieze. The perspective is such that it makes her appear all the more otherworldly.

The drawing, in particular of the figure, is carefully representational, although the pencil lines almost disappear against the bright colours of the foreground and the delicate tones of the sky. Mackintosh painted this as he was becoming more involved with the Macdonald sisters and Herbert McNair. As they developed their own 'Spook School' style, his paintings were to become much more abstract and difficult to interpret.

His later works, such as *Cabbages in an Orchard*, were hardly understood at the time without Mackintosh's accompanying explanatory text. *The Shadow – The Tree of Influence* and *The Tree of Personal Effort* are even more obscure, the symbolic forms defying interpretation by anyone outside the Four. The theme of nature and otherworldliness had been part of a fad which, growing from and combined with spiritualism, had gained enough credence in America to have provoked serious debates in the Senate. Indeed, at one time the American Spiritualist League had been led by a woman who was to be the first to stand for president of the United States, Victoria Woodhull. She had moved to England at the beginning of the 20th century.

Although spiritualism had long lost its appeal among the fashionable set, the notion of natural forces being greater and more spiritually powerful than any belief system invented by man had gained enough credence to influence poetry, dance and music. By employing natural, spiritual themes, the Four were being contemporary and slightly risqué.

# THE TREE OF INFLUENCE – THE TREE OF IMPORTANCE – THE SUN OF COWARDICE *1895*

*Courtesy of the Glasgow School of Art Collection*

THE *Tree of Influence – The Tree of Importance – The Sun of Cowardice* is one of a pair of Symbolist watercolours that Mackintosh painted in 1895. They appeared in *The Magazine*, a handwritten publication produced by a group of students, the Immortals, containing watercolours, fairy tales, drawings and commentaries. However, there was no accompanying text to these two paintings and no one has been able to explain exactly what Mackintosh meant by them. It is possible that they allude to subjects discussed by the readers of *The Magazine* and it is certain that they could be interpreted though the private Symbolist vocabulary of the Four.

At this period in their lives, the Macdonald sisters' work was as important as Mackintosh's and their distinctive paintings also appeared in *The Magazine*. One of the many influences behind these paintings was the Glasgow Boys, a group of local painters enthusiastically supported by Francis Newbery, director of the Glasgow School of Art. George Henry and E. A. Hornel collaborated on two paintings that have resonances in the work of the Four. Their *The Druids* (1890) and *Star in the East* (1891) combined mysterious imagery and ornate Celtic decoration with bright colours touched with gold, and provided inspiration for many artists working in Glasgow at the time.

The Four were also aware of the work of Aubrey Beardsley, the Pre-Raphaelites, especially Burne-Jones and Rossetti, and the Dutch painter Jan Toorop. Newbery possessed a copy of Zola's *Le Rêve* which included illustrations by Carlos Schwabe, another rich source of inspiration. These were the origins of the distinctive technique which became known as the Glasgow Style. Its most typical practitioners were the Four and its influence spread among a wide group of designers, architects and craftsmen.

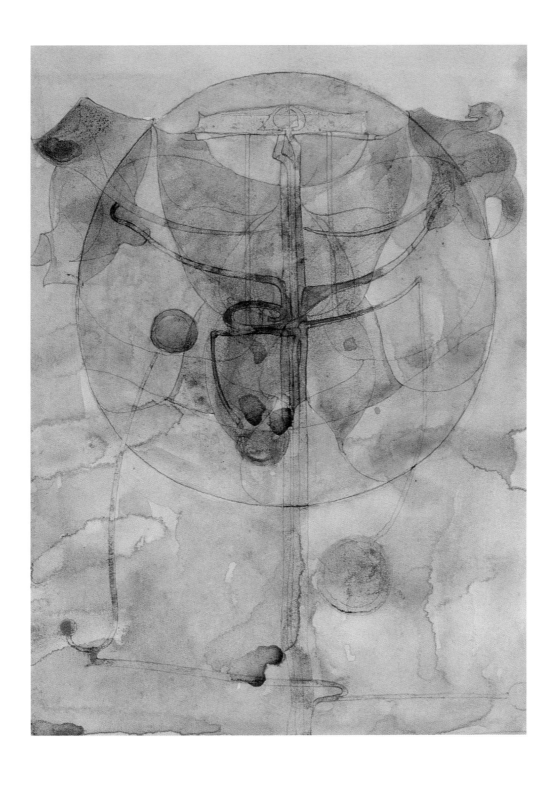

## POSTER FOR THE SCOTTISH MUSICAL REVIEW *1896*

*Courtesy of the Hunterian Art Gallery, University of Glasgow*

HAVING completed a considerable number of watercolours, the Four turned to poster designs. Over seven feet high, with their own peculiarly distinctive images and lettering, whose attention would not be caught by them? And what better opportunity could there be to advertise simultaneously one's own presence in the design world?

Mackintosh produced four posters, of which this is the most arresting. It features a sinister stylised woman with four birds beside her. She is dressed in a long dark cloak, her head is silhouetted against a large halo, and a decorative system of lines frame her and mysteriously pierce three circular symbols above her head. The colours are sombre, black and deep indigo, but pierced with the red and green dots of the birds' wings and tail feathers and of the discs on high.

The typography of the poster is certainly idiosyncratic, as it was on all the posters the Four designed. Although these posters were greeted with outrage, Gleeson White, editor of *The Studio*, defended them, pointing out that the aim of a poster was to attract attention: 'Mr Mackintosh's posters may be somewhat trying to the average person...But there is so much decorative method in his perversion of humanity that despite all the ridicule and abuse it has excited, it is possible to defend his treatment.'

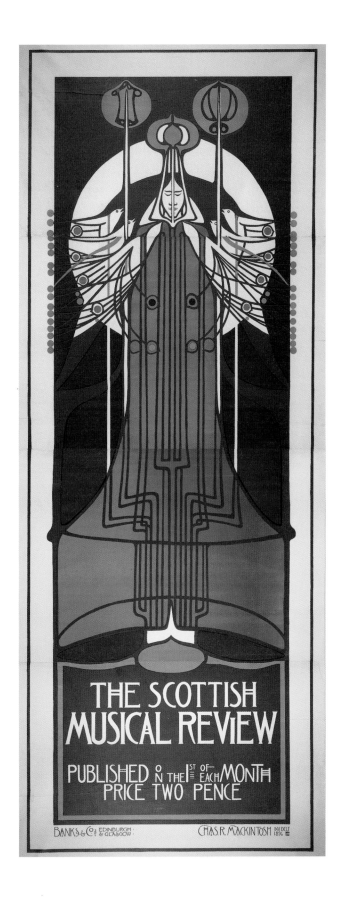

# LARKSPUR *1914*

*Courtesy of the Hunterian Art Gallery, University of Glasgow*

BY 1914 Mackintosh was in the grip of depression. He was drinking heavily and was known to be acerbic and arrogant, demanding the highest standards from his workmen but constantly changing the details of work in progress. In 1913 he had resigned from his position at Honeyman and Keppie and set up his own office, but work was scarce and nobody offered him a commission. Rumours circulated about him, discrediting both his character and his work. Naturally he felt low in confidence and in need of respite from the pressures of city life and work. The trip to Suffolk came at a most opportune moment, even affording him, as it did, the false notion of it being a 'work' trip.

In the summer, he and Margaret holidayed in Walberswick, Suffolk. Mackintosh's old friend and mentor Francis Newbery had a semidetached house there and the Mackintoshes rented the one next door. All his life Mackintosh had sketched wild flowers when travelling and now was no exception. He began to work on 40 illustrations of wild flowers for a book that was – despite the impending onset of the Great War at the time of commission – to be published in Germany. Unfortunately, because of the war it would never appear.

Over the years, as one can see, his flower drawings had become more stylised. *Larkspur* shows how Mackintosh drew the flower from every angle in pencil and then used a colour wash with some solid colour to pick out particular details. The attention to the natural light and how colours appear in the natural world is clearly noted.

The box contains information as to the place and date the picture was made, and also the initials of Mackintosh and Margaret. This does not necessarily indicate Margaret's collaboration in the drawing, however, simply that she was present when it was done.

# FRITILLARIA *1915*

*Courtesy of the Hunterian Art Gallery, University of Glasgow*

WHEN the Mackintoshes went to Walberswick, it seems they had no intention of leaving Glasgow for good. However, Suffolk proved to be so popular with artists and so congenial that Margaret returned briefly to Glasgow just to let Florentine Terrace so that Mackintosh could continue to rest and recover his confidence.

His style of flower drawing developed greatly in this period, possibly because he could see the works as part of a book and so had a focus to his work. In *Fritillaria*, the style is more defined, the flower placed carefully in the centre of the page, almost as if he was drawing a botanical specimen. The result is certainly more figurative than any previous such work by Mackintosh.

His use of colour is much more specific, used clearly to define the parts of the flower. The chequered petals must have appealed to him, as they echoed so much of his designs for stencils and allowed him the mathematical reference he so enjoyed developing in much of his design. The presence of such order in the natural world can possibly have provided more proof and validation of how he worked, too. He paints them with great care, even repeating them in the label.

Mackintosh always drew freshly cut flowers when he was in Walberswick. He most likely wandered the country lanes looking for them or asking for specimens from people's gardens. This is Constable country, remember, so had a painterly familiarity about it which could have inspired the artist in him. He must have cut a strange figure, however, as he stooped along lanes in his long cape and deerstalker, sketchbook and pencil in hand, with his unfamiliar accent.

# JAPANESE WITCH HAZEL *1915*

*Courtesy of the Hunterian Art Gallery, University of Glasgow*

MACKINTOSH'S exquisite flower pictures owe something to Japanese art, which he and Margaret enjoyed for many years. There is often a strong Oriental influence in his graphics and this flat style of representation is directly linked with Japanese drawings. *Japanese Witch Hazel*, like his other plant drawings, has a two-dimensional quality. It is perhaps odd that Mackintosh should adopt this style, since architecture is concerned with three dimensions and the play of light and shade. The completely featureless background and the absence of light and shade show he deliberately made no attempt at three-dimensional representation. This contrast between the plain background and the intricacy of the piece is within the spirit of Aubrey Beardsley and some of Whistler's paintings. However, it is enlivened here by the way the stems cross over each other.

The colour is secondary to Mackintosh's enjoyment of the decorative shapes made by the delicate twisted petals. However, it shows less spontaneity in its artistry than some of the flower paintings of just the previous year. Unfortunately, his time in Walberswick was limited. It was discovered that he was corresponding with Austria and Germany. The fact that his correspondents were fellow architects, designers and friends was considered irrelevant. Mackintosh was accused of being a spy and ordered to appear before a tribunal. Both he and Margaret, patriots to the last, were devastated by this turn of affairs. Determined to clear his name, he went to London, where with the help of Sir Patrick Geddes's daughter the War Office was persuaded of his innocence. Margaret moved to join him and they settled in London, never to return to Suffolk again.

# PINKS *c.1922–3*

*Courtesy of Glasgow Museums*

THE Mackintoshes settled in a studio apartment in Glebe Place, Chelsea, where they rented two studios next door. Here they found themselves in the company of fellow artists, meeting with them frequently in the evenings when dining at the Blue Cockatoo. They made many friends, among them Augustus John, Margaret Morris, J. D. Fergusson, Randolph Schwabe and James Stewart Hill.

Unsuprisingly perhaps, they thrived in these avant-garde, bohemian circles. However, the demands of war meant there was little or no architectural work to be had, so Mackintosh and Margaret turned to textile design and, in his case, flower painting. But now his style changed, most probably because of commercial considerations and the demands of popular taste. Instead of fresh flowers, he turned to cultivated ones arranged in a vase. Often he did not use a specific setting but relied on the interest provided by the jug or vase, neither of which overwhelmed the flowers themselves.

Mackintosh's botanical knowledge is once more evident here, but the paintings are much richer than his Walberswick watercolours, often with tonal variations and colour harmonies that relate to his textile designs. Clearly Mackintosh was feeling more positive toward the idea of painting for a living when working on this series of watercolours. The overall effect is of a stronger, more powerful image.

Sometimes he added backgrounds which might feature his own textile designs, as in *Anemones* (*c.*1916), or a table with chequered tablecloth in *White Tulips* (*c.*1918–20). Once, in *Yellow Tulips* (*c.*1922–3), in a rare move for Mackintosh, we are even allowed a glimpse of his Chelsea home.

## TEXTILE DESIGNS *1915–23*

### TENDRILS, SQUARES AND TRIANGLES;
### STYLISED PLANT FORM, BLACK PURPLE, GREEN & PINK

*Courtesy of the Hunterian Art Gallery, University of Glasgow*

TEXTILE design was a new departure for Mackintosh that served to supplement his meagre income while he was in London during the war years. Until now he had produced only stencilled or embroidered patterns on fabric that played a specific role within a particular interior, such as the chair-back in the Rose Boudoir or the fabric on the settle in the Hill House's white bedroom.

None of these were intended for mass production. However, between 1915 and 1923 Mackintosh produced over 120 different designs for commercial use, ranging from representational or stylised flower patterns to more abstract geometric motifs in both dynamic and subtle colours. The patterns were bought principally by William Foxton's or Sefton's.

There are, unfortunately, no records showing exactly which of Mackintosh's many designs were produced, and only a few samples have survived. Much of his textile work was inspired by Viennese design, as well as the more avant-garde movements in the contemporary art world – for example, post-Impressionism, Fauvism and Vorticism. Sometimes he specified which fabrics would suit which designs, so it can be assumed they were used for clothing as well as furnishing fabrics.

Although apparently a long way from his original calling as an architect, this sort of designing suited the way he saw two-dimensional pattern.

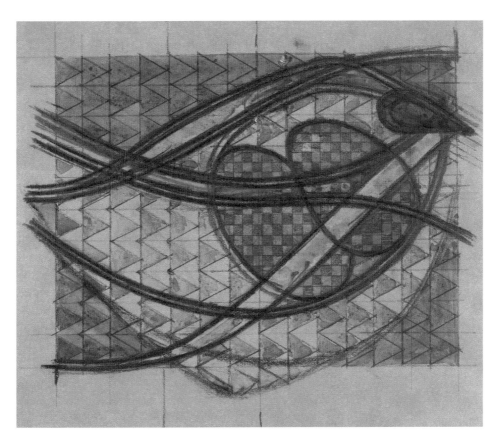

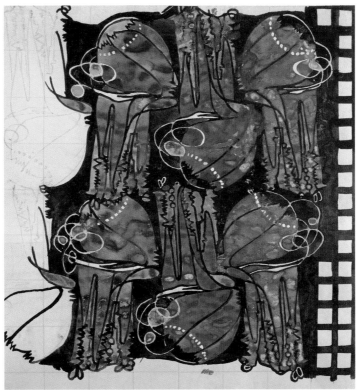

# THE VILLAGE OF LA LAGONNE *c. 1924–7*

*Courtesy of Glasgow Museums*

EVEN after the war architectural commissions proved hard to find. Mackintosh was struggling to make a living and it looked unlikely that he would ever be able to set up an architectural practice of his own. He was cut off from his Glaswegian contacts and had failed to make many in London. He was depressed, so friends encouraged him to take a break.

In 1923 he and Margaret embarked on a holiday that was in the end to last four years. They travelled to the South of France, to the point where Roussillon meets the Pyrenees. Initially they moved about from town to town – Amélie-les-Bains, Île-sur-Tête, Port Vendres and Mont Louis – relishing the simple life, walking, reading, sampling the regional food and wine and, of course, painting. Mackintosh embarked on a new body of work whose principal subject was the landscape around him. Frequently he would seek to highlight the relationship of a town with its natural surroundings – a theme he had explored with building design work, furniture design and decorative flourishes in work such as that in the Salon de Luxe.

The village of La Lagonne was in easy reach of Mont Louis, where they liked to retreat from the heat of the summer sun. Mackintosh preferred to paint in the open only when the sun was shining, having spent time analysing the subject first. He concentrated on the use of colour, shape, tone and line to recreate an essentially architectural vision dependent, as so much of his architectural work was, on the play of real, available light. Strangely alienating in composition, this is a world empty of people where the artist can make patterns from the fields, the rooftops and the strangely two-dimensional rocky outcrop in the centre of the picture.

# LE FORT MAILLERT *1927*

*Courtesy of the Glasgow School of Art Collection*

WHILE Margaret was away in London, Mackintosh painted two extraordinary rock studies, *Le Fort Maillert* and *The Rock*. The first did not take him as long to finish as *The Rock* and when it was nearly complete he wrote to Margaret, referring to it as 'our fort'. It has been suggested that they were particularly attached to it because of its resemblance to the castle on Holy Island, where the Mackintoshes spent their honeymoon in 1900.

What is so striking about the painting is the sheer monumentality of the rock face beneath the fort itself. Mackintosh adds to the dramatic effect by choosing to paint it from below so the rock looms threateningly upwards, overpowering the picture. Once more he reveals his constant interest in architectural shapes, detailing the formations and cracks, the quality of the stone, the light and shade, while retaining a flat, almost two-dimensional quality. The fort seems incidental to the rocks but echoes their sense of mass and permanence under the brilliant blue sky.

These paintings were not quick to complete, it appears. Mackintosh's letters to Margaret are evidence of weeks of painstaking progress as he struggled with his subject, anxious to get the detail and colour exactly right. As with his painting of La Lagonne, there are no human forms visible here, and no sign of life at all. It is as if he has purged himself of any desire to recreate the flower and fauna of the natural world, and instead gone toward the hard, harsh lines of the least yielding natural things. In painting rock, of course, Mackintosh is interacting with the very raw materials from which his early work is hewn, but in a far more passive manner. This work could be interpreted as a statement of his accession to the power of nature over his ability to work with or against it. Here he is not building, creating and physically interacting with the rock, but merely reporting it as he finds it. There is a certain awe displayed in the towering mass that confronts the artist, acceptance of its finality and power.

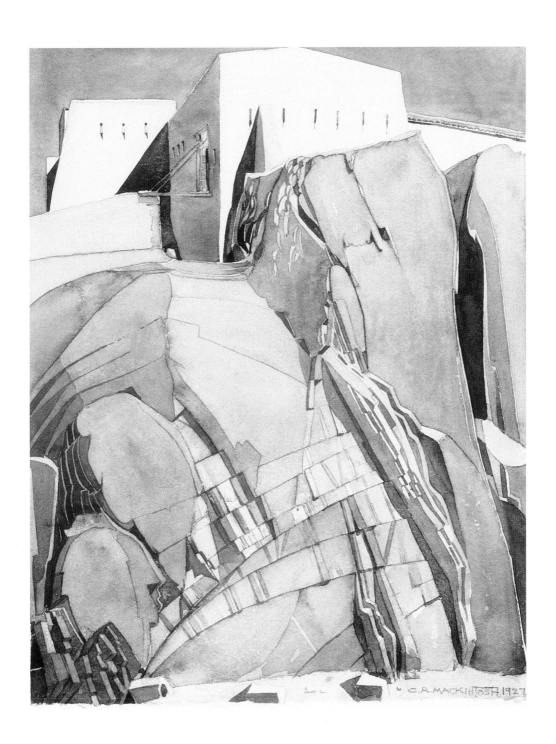

# La Rue du Soleil, Port Vendres *1926*

*Courtesy of the Hunterian Art Gallery, University of Glasgow*

THIS is perhaps the most dramatic of all the pictures Mackintosh painted of Port Vendres. The small fishing village sits brooding above the sea wall but the focus of the picture is on the shimmering mass of reflected and refracted light frozen in the water below. What is striking is the overwhelming sense of design that dominates the picture, the sea having almost been reduced to abstraction.

Mackintosh is, once again, unconcerned with human activity or mood. These pictures portray a static, unpeopled world where he can devise patterns without compromising the identity of the place. He explored neither the location nor his reactions to it. Instead, his fascination was with what was permanent in the landscape; painting seems, in this way, another aspect of his architecture, or at least a way for him to still connect to it.

Mackintosh appears to have used the minimum of equipment, which allowed him to scramble unencumbered to the best vantage points. Once he had established his position, he would make an architectural sketch of the scene in pencil, then paint it in, erasing the pencil marks as he worked. From letters and surviving literature we know that Mackintosh worked hard at his paintings, sometimes taking a fortnight or more to complete one. It is clear he enjoyed playing the same games with space and light as he did in the best of his architectural designs, massing forms together to achieve a bold elemental effect. Interestingly, here he plays games with the reflection of light and not the man-made structures opposite his position. They are, for the most part, unremarkable buildings constructed for function, not form. The line and shape of the sea wall is the only part of the human-made landscape with which Mackintosh seems to exercise artistic license. Its line echoes those of the hills beyond the village.

# THE LITTLE BAY, PORT VENDRES *1927*

*Courtesy of the Hunterian Art Gallery, University of Glasgow*

IN May 1927 Margaret had to return to London for medical treatment. Mackintosh wrote her long letters, detailing how he spent his time, the weather, the food, his problem in introducing more light into his pictures, his concern with his overuse of green paint and his experimentation with style. *The Little Bay*, typically painted from a high vantage point for dramatic effect, is another essay in immobility. He is unconcerned with any human activity or local colour. The strong blues of the sky and sea contrast with the earth colours of the townscape and contribute to the heavy sense of heat and stillness at midday.

The emphasis of the picture is on the architectural composition of the whole and the linear patterns within it. The stark contrast between the vibrant, living blue of the sky and sea and the grey, man-made buildings hints at a kind of coming to terms with how his battle against nature has fared. There are echoes of a kind of sense of failure in this series of paintings. As an architect Charles Rennie Mackintosh had attempted to make buildings live, grow and become modern. He had put tributes to the power and beauty of nature in his buildings. These paintings are his way of stating that man could never match nature and that, in fact, he generally ends up making a mess. Mackintosh's alienation from his fellow man is conveyed by the lack of any human forms in these paintings.

Port Vendres was one of the places where Mackintosh whiled away lonely hours, watching the activity in the harbour. He began to write to Margaret about soreness in his tongue, which he blamed on the American tobacco sold in France. However, at the end of the year after Margaret's return, he became seriously ill. They at last came back to London, where he was diagnosed as suffering from cancer of the tongue. After radiotherapy he was left virtually unable to speak.

Charles Rennie Mackintosh died in a nursing home in December 1928.

# GLOSSARY

**architrave** The moulded frame surrounding a door or a window.

**Art Deco** Style of art and decoration popular in Europe and America in the 1920s and 1930s. Named after the 1925 Paris Exposition Internationale des Arts Décoratifs et Industriels Modernes and characterised by strong colours and geometric shapes.

**Art Nouveau** Style of art and decoration popular at the end of the 19th century, characterised by use of natural motifs and sinuous, undulating lines.

**Arts and Crafts movement** A late-19th-century English movement which aimed to revive handicrafts and transform architecture by using traditional building methods and local materials.

**cantilever** A beam that projects horizontally from a wall to support something above it such as a balcony.

**chamfer** The surface made when an edge is rounded off or bevelled at a 45-degree angle.

**coffer** A hollowed-out square in a ceiling.

**corbel** A block that projects from a wall to support a beam or upper level.

**cornice** 1. Decorative moulded plaster work that runs round edge of ceiling. 2. A projecting moulding at the summit of an outside wall.

**dado rail** Divides different parts of the wall when they are decorated differently.

**eaves** The underneath of a roof that overhangs the wall.

**egg and dart** A pattern based on alternating egg shapes and arrows.

**Fauvism** Early-20th-century movement in French art which used colour for pure decoration or to communicate emotion.

**flying buttress** A structure built against a building or projecting from it which gives added support.

**Four, the** The group made up of Frances and Margaret Macdonald, Charles Rennie Mackintosh and Herbert McNair who developed a distinctive symbolic vocabulary and style of representation.

**Free Style** A term used to describe the work of late-19th-century architects such as Web, Shaw and Ashby who mixed elements of classical architecture with vernacular features in an unorthodox manner.

**frieze rail** A decorative strip running along a wall.

**gable** 1. The triangular upper part of a side wall between the twin slopes of a pitched roof. 2. The triangular canopy above a door or window.

**gesso** Plaster used for moulds, casts and as a medium for sculpture.

**Glasgow Boys, the** A group of painters working in Glasgow during the late 19th century.

**Glasgow Style** A style of art common to local Glaswegian artists working in the late 19th century which featured a particular linearity, stylised organic motifs and a mysterious, ethereal atmosphere.

**Gothic** A style of European architecture popular between the 12th and 16th centuries, featuring pointed arches, flying buttresses and vaulted ceilings.

**Greek Revival** see Neoclassicism

**harling** pebbledash or roughcast

**Immortals, the** A self-styled group of women students at the Glasgow School of Art during the 1860s.

**inglenook** A corner or recess within a large open fireplace.

**joist** A beam supporting a floor or ceiling.

**keystone** The central supporting stone at the crown of an arch.

**latticework** An open frame made of crossed horizontal and vertical strips of wood or metal.

**lintel** Stone or wooden horizontal beam across the top of a doorway.

**loggia** A roofed gallery or room open to the outside on one or more sides.

**Mannerism** A style of architecture favoured in 16th-century France, Spain and Italy, principally using *trompe l'oeil* effects and classical elements.

**maquette** A preliminary model made by a sculptor, usually in wax, clay or plaster.

**modernism** Term used for 20th-century avant-garde experimentation in various art forms, characterised by asymmetry, lack of ornamentation, unrelieved geometric shapes, open plans and white rendering.

**mullion** The vertical divide that separates the panes of glass in a window.

**Neoclassicism** A classical revival that took place from the 1750s as a reaction to the excesses of the Baroque and Rococo styles that preceded it. It was characterised by simplicity of form and lack of decoration.

**newel post** The posts at the top and bottom of a flight of stairs that support the banister rail.

**ogee** An S-shaped curve.

**oriel** A bay window that is supported and ornamented by corbels.

**pediment** A low-pitched triangular gable set over a portico, door or window.

**pilaster** A rectangular pillar that slightly projects from a wall.

**portico** Covered entrance or porch.

**post-Impressionism** A term used to describe more progressive types of French painting since the1880s.

**Pre-Raphaelites** A group of artists formed in London in 1848 who proposed to transform Victorian art with their return to fidelity to nature and colour.

**relief** A sculpture where the figures stand out from the background.

**reveal** The part of a wall which lies between a window or door and the outer wall surface.

**sash** One of two sliding panes that make up one window.

**sconce** A bracket attached to a wall, holding a candle or light.

**Scottish baronial** A style of architecture developed for Scottish country houses from the 1830s.

**Spook School** The term used to describe the work of the Four because of its ghostly, weird nature.

**stretcher** A horizontal piece of wood between the legs of a chair or table that gives added strength.

**Symbolism** A 19th-century movement in the arts which used symbols to convey meaning.

**tie beam** A beam that runs between two rafters to ensure they remain in position.

**truss** The metal or wooden framework that supports the roof.

**vernacular** A term denoting indigenous styles of buildings made in local materials following traditional methods of construction.

**Vienna Secession** A group of artists and architects who broke away from the Künstlerhaus, the conservative academy in Vienna, to forge an influential new style.

**Vorticism** A movement in English art which began in 1913, inspired by the Futurists.

**ziggurat** A pyramid-like tower that was built in stages, the best known being the Tower of Babel and the one at Ur.

# FURTHER READING

Billcliffe, Roger *Mackintosh Watercolours* (John Murray, London, 1978).

*Mackintosh Furniture* (Lutterworth Press, Cambridge, 1984).

Buchanan, William, ed. *Mackintosh's Masterwork: The Glasgow School of Art* (Chambers, Edinburgh, 1994).

Crawford, Alan *Charles Rennie Mackintosh* (Thames & Hudson, London, 1995).

Fiell, Charlotte and Peter *Charles Rennie Mackintosh* (Benedikt Taschen Verlag, Köln, 1995).

Grigg, Jocelyn *Charles Rennie Mackintosh* (Richard Drew Publishing Ltd, Glasgow, 1987).

Hackney, Iona and Isla *Charles Rennie Mackintosh* (The Apple Press, London, 1989).

Kaplan, Wendy, ed. *Charles Rennie Mackintosh* (Abbeville Press, New York, 1996).

McKean, John, and Baxter, Colin *Charles Rennie Mackintosh* (Colin Baxter Photography Ltd, Moray, 1998).

Wilhide, Elizabeth *The Mackintosh Style: Decor & Design* (Pavilion, London, 1995).